Praise for *Motherland Lost*

In *Motherland Lost*, his superb new book, Sam Tadros presents two stories, combined and intertwined, necessarily so but with no sacrifice of skill and elegance. One story is the history of the ancient Coptic Church from its origins in Egypt in the first century down to the present day. This important and noble story is regrettably little known in the West. With this book it should be no longer. The other story is the history of Egypt, especially the history of its encounter with modernity, which, as Tadros shows, cannot be understood apart from the fate of the Coptic Church. This fate has not been happy and is getting worse under the impact of the Egyptian Revolution of 2011. Though it belies the hopes invested in those events, it is indispensable to their interpretation for anyone seeking to understand the "new" Egypt.

—HILLEL FRADKIN, Hudson Institute

Motherland Lost is a history written with sophistication—and with tears. Samuel Tadros tells the story of Egypt's failed attempts at modernization in the last century and explains how even the movements that seemed liberal meant danger for Egypt's Copts. From Nasser to Sadat to today's Muslim Brotherhood regime, the Copts have faced narrowing public space—and today's Islamists threaten to force them into second-class status with a future Tadros describes as "bleak." Today emigration is turning the Coptic Church, Tadros explains, into a global entity with hundreds of churches and schools around the world but threatening its survival where it emerged millennia ago—as the Egyptian state, Islamists in power, and violent mobs combine to bring the future of Copts in Egypt into doubt. To understand Egypt's past and the challenges that cloud its future, this book is essential.

—ELLIOTT ABRAMS, Council on Foreign Relations

Samuel Tadros has written an essential history of an important subject. In crisp prose and with an eye for the interesting detail, he tells the remarkable and little-known history of a people and a church that have been integral to Egypt for two thousand years. Today, with the Copts in peril as almost never before in their own land, it's critical that this story be understood. We're fortunate that Tadros explains it so well.

—BRET STEPHENS, *Wall Street Journal*

Motherland Lost

The Egyptian and
Coptic Quest for Modernity

HERBERT AND JANE DWIGHT WORKING GROUP ON ISLAMISM AND THE INTERNATIONAL ORDER

Motherland Lost

The Egyptian and Coptic Quest for Modernity

Samuel Tadros

HOOVER INSTITUTION PRESS

STANFORD UNIVERSITY | STANFORD, CALIFORNIA

www.hoover.org

Hoover Institution Press Publication No. 638

Hoover Institution at Leland Stanford Junior University, Stanford, California 94305-6010

First printing 2013
21 20 19 18 17 16 15 14 13   9 8 7 6 5 4 3 2

Manufactured in the United States of America

The paper used in this publication meets the minimum Requirements of the American National Standard for Information Sciences—Permanence of Paper for Printed Library Materials, ANSI/NISO Z39.48-1992. ⊗

Cataloging-in-Publication Data is available from the Library of Congress.
ISBN 978-0-8179-1644-2 (cloth : alk. paper)
ISBN 978-0-8179-1646-6 (e-book)
ISBN 978-0-8179-1647-3 (mobi)
ISBN 978-0-8179-1648-0 (pdf)

HOOVER
INSTITUTION
STANFORD
UNIVERSITY

*The Hoover Institution gratefully acknowledges
the following individuals and foundations
for their significant support of the*

HERBERT AND JANE DWIGHT WORKING GROUP
ON ISLAMISM AND THE INTERNATIONAL ORDER:

Herbert and Jane Dwight

Beall Family Foundation

Stephen Bechtel Foundation

Lynde and Harry Bradley Foundation

Mr. and Mrs. Clayton W. Frye Jr.

Lakeside Foundation

To Laila:
May she grow proud of the heritage of her ancestors
and aware of the price they paid to offer it to her.

CONTENTS

F OR DECADES, THE THEMES of the Hoover Institution
have revolved around the broad concerns of political and
economic and individual freedom. The Cold War that
engaged and challenged our nation during the twentieth century
guided a good deal of Hoover's work, including its archival accumulation and research studies. The steady output of work on the
communist world offers durable testimonies to that time, and
struggle. But there is no repose from history's exertions, and no
sooner had communism left the stage of history than a huge challenge arose in the broad lands of the Islamic world. A brief respite,
and a meandering road, led from the fall of the Berlin Wall on 11/9
in 1989 to 9/11. Hoover's project, the Herbert and Jane Dwight
Working Group on Islamism and the International Order, is our
contribution to a deeper understanding of the struggle in the
Islamic world between order and its nemesis, between Muslims
keen to protect the rule of reason and the gains of modernity, and
those determined to deny the Islamic world its place in the modern international order of states. The United States is deeply
engaged, and dangerously exposed, in the Islamic world, and we see
our working group as part and parcel of the ongoing confrontation
with the radical Islamists who have declared war on the states in
their midst, on American power and interests, and on the very
order of the international state system.

The Islamists are doubtless a minority in the world of Islam.
But they are a determined breed. Their world is the Islamic emir-
ate, led by self-styled "emirs and mujahedeen in the path of God"

and legitimized by the pursuit of the caliphate that collapsed with the end of the Ottoman Empire in 1924. These masters of terror and their foot soldiers have made it increasingly difficult to integrate the world of Islam into modernity. In the best of worlds, the entry of Muslims into modern culture and economics would have presented difficulties of no small consequence: the strictures on women, the legacy of humiliation and self-pity, the outdated educational systems, and an explosive demography that is forever at war with social and economic gains. But the borders these warriors of the faith have erected between Islam and "the other" are particularly forbidding. The lands of Islam were the lands of a crossroads civilization, trading routes and mixed populations. The Islamists have waged war, and a brutally effective one it has to be conceded, against that civilizational inheritance. The leap into the modern world economy as attained by China and India in recent years will be virtually impossible in a culture that feeds off belligerent self-pity, and endlessly calls for wars of faith.

The war of ideas with radical Islamism is inescapably central to this Hoover endeavor. The strategic context of this clash, the landscape of that Greater Middle East, is the other pillar. We face three layers of danger in the heartland of the Islamic world: states that have succumbed to the sway of terrorists in which state authority no longer exists (Afghanistan, Somalia, and Yemen), dictatorial regimes that suppress their people at home and pursue deadly weapons of mass destruction and adventurism abroad (Iraq under Saddam Hussein, the Iranian theocracy), and "enabler" regimes, such as the ones in Egypt and Saudi Arabia, which export their own problems with radical Islamism to other parts of the Islamic world and beyond. In this context, the task of reversing Islamist radicalism and of reforming and strengthening the state across the entire Muslim world—the Middle East, Africa, as well as South, Southeast, and Central Asia—is the greatest strategic challenge of the twenty-first century. The essential starting point is detailed knowledge of our enemy.

Thus, the working group will draw on the intellectual resources of Hoover and Stanford and on an array of scholars and practitioners from elsewhere in the United States from the Middle East and the broader world of Islam. The scholarship on contemporary Islam can now be read with discernment. A good deal of it, produced in the immediate aftermath of 9/11, was not particularly deep and did not stand the test of time and events. We, however, are in the favorable position of a "second generation" assessment of that Islamic material. Our scholars and experts can report, in a detailed, authoritative way, on Islam within the Arabian Peninsula, on trends within Egyptian Islam, on the struggle between the Kemalist secular tradition in Turkey and the new Islamists, particularly the fight for the loyalty of European Islam between those who accept the canon, and the discipline, of modernism and those who do not.

Arabs and Muslims need not be believers in American exceptionalism, but our hope is to engage them in this contest of ideas. We will not necessarily aim at producing primary scholarship, but such scholarship may materialize in that our participants are researchers who know their subjects intimately. We see our critical output as essays accessible to a broader audience, primers about matters that require explication, op-eds, writings that will become part of the public debate, and short, engaging books that can illuminate the choices and the struggles in modern Islam.

We see this endeavor as a faithful reflection of the values that animate a decent, moderate society. We know the travails of modern Islam, and this working group will be unsparing in depicting them. But we also know that the battle for modern Islam is not yet lost, that there are brave men and women fighting to retrieve their faith from the extremists. Some of our participants will themselves be intellectuals and public figures who have stood up to the pressure. The working group will be unapologetic about America's role in the Muslim world. A power that laid to waste religious tyranny in Afghanistan and despotism in Iraq, that came to the rescue of the Muslims in the Balkans when they appeared all but doomed, has given much to those burdened populations. We haven't always understood Islam and Muslims—hence this inquiry. But it is a given of the working group that the pursuit of modernity and human welfare, and of the rule of law and reason, in Islamic lands is the common ground between America and contemporary Islam.

FOUAD AJAMI
Senior Fellow, Hoover Institution—
Cochairman, Herbert and Jane Dwight Working Group
on Islamism and the International Order

CHARLES HILL
Distinguished Fellow of the Brady-Johnson Program
in Grand Strategy at Yale University;
Research Fellow, Hoover Institution—
Cochairman, Herbert and Jane Dwight Working Group
on Islamism and the International Order

THEIR WIDE-EYED FACES LOOK AT US INTENTLY, curiously, sometimes welcoming, sometimes stern, always alert. These antique portraits of the Copts of Egypt on intricately woven textiles are a cultural treasure for the whole world, visible testimony that all humanity, from the dawn of time to our time is one. "Deep is the well of the past," the novelist proclaimed, "shall we not call it bottomless?"[1] To be true to itself a society—every society—must create a partnership among its past, present, and future. There is no true Egypt without the Coptic Christians. The numerical concept of "a minority" does not apply to an inextricable element of a people's soul.

The place of the Copts in the state may be the most ultimately consequential mission facing Egypt today. Success or failure will lap the shores of waters far beyond the Nile, farther beyond even the Arab-Islamic realms. The system by which nations have agreed to structure their relations, address common problems, and search for a stable, mutually productive future founds itself on an acceptance of inclusiveness. If one precept explains the extent to which any such thing as an "international community" can be contemplated, it is that to be a member in good standing, a good international "citizen," means to mutually recognize, accept, and interweave the multiplicity of strands making up the human fabric.

Like the fifth-century Christian Augustine, the twelfth-century Muslim Averroes (Ibn Rushd) saw wisdom in Plato's depiction of

---

1. Thomas Mann, *Joseph and His Brothers*.

a "statesman" as one skilled in the practical art of weaving. The richly colored, complexly woven textiles from which those ancient yet familiar expressions gaze out at us are revelations of what the governance of a state must do to be legitimate and successful in our time. All who want to understand the challenge need to read this book.

CHARLES HILL
Distinguished Fellow of the Brady-Johnson Program
in Grand Strategy at Yale University;
Research Fellow, Hoover Institution—
Cochairman, Herbert and Jane Dwight Working Group
on Islamism and the International Order
February 27, 2013

ACKNOWLEDGMENTS

IT WAS NEARLY A YEAR AND A HALF AGO that I received a
phone call from Fouad Ajami asking me whether I would be
interested in writing a book about Egypt and its Copts. The
idea was both appealing and unsettling. To be asked by a man you
admire so much to write your first book as part of a series with so
many acclaimed authors is enough to fill any man's heart with joy,
but the Coptic question was one that I had tried to avoid through
most of my life. My rebellious years had taken me to places far
away from the Copts and their plight, first to the dreams of Arab
nationalism and then to the false confidence of liberalism. Like
Sophocles's tragic hero, I had left Corinth seeking an escape from
my fate not realizing that it awaited me in Thebes.

Leo Strauss has described liberal education as "liberation from
vulgarity." "The Greeks," he wrote, "had a beautiful word for 'vulgarity'; they called it *apeirokalia*, lack of experience in things beautiful." Researching and writing this book was indeed a form of
liberal education—a liberation from the vulgarity of the daily
political developments in Egypt and an experience in things that
are no less beautiful by virtue of being painful. I am indebted to
Fouad not only for his initial leap of faith, but for his endless support, encouragement, and kindness through the whole process.
Though not fortunate to be his student, he is nonetheless my
mo'allem.

I was fortunate to have in Megan Ring an amazing friend at
Hoover. In one of our first introductory emails, she described her-
self as from now on "your person in Hoover." I wouldn't have had

it any other way. I would like to thank Charles Hill for his support and the Hoover Institution Press team for making this book a reality, especially Susan Edmiston for her editing.

But the educational journey had started long before that phone call. As a child I sat for endless hours listening to my father's stories and pressing him for more. He had known the founding fathers of the Coptic Church's revival, named me after one of them, and his stories and books introduced me to the history of an ancient church, its glorious moments as well as its failings. But if it was my father's books and stories that gave me my first lessons of the church, so was I taught to love it by my mother.

Amr Bargisi helped me think through my arguments, criticized and refined them. In hundreds of conversations, in his invaluable insights, with his continuous support he has fulfilled the offices of friendship and beyond. Mourad Takawi lent me his unpublished thesis as well as his ears and mind for countless hours discussing the book's chapters. Rami Wasfi and Maged Atiya read the complete manuscript and offered their comments. It is a better book because of all of them and I am grateful for their support and suggestions.

I am grateful for the support of my colleagues and friends at the Hudson Institute. The Hudson Institute is a place dedicated to innovative research and it has given me the intellectual freedom necessary to research and write. I am proud to call it home. I am particularly grateful to the support of Ken Weinstein, Lewis Libby, Abram Shulsky, Eric Brown, Paul Marshall, Lela Gilbert, and Kurt Werthmuller. I would like to especially thank Nina Shea, to whom I am indebted for her continuous encouragement for this book, as well as for so many other things. I have been blessed with the friendship of Hillel Fradkin who offered me his professional and personal support.

I would like to thank Elliott Abrams, whom I was fortunate to have as a professor and more fortunate to know as a friend, as well as Bret Stephens, whose support has not diminished since I first met him six years ago, for their blurbs for this book.

It is common for an author to conclude his acknowledgments by thanking his wife, but Rania's role has been anything but common. This book would not have been written if not for her unlimited support and encouragement. She endured the long process of researching and writing, lifted me up when the news from Egypt was too much to bear, and pushed me forward when I faltered. Her faith in me kept me going and she was and is my rock.

Confucius said that "you cannot open a book without learning something." It occurs to me that writing a book multiplies the learning process, not merely about abstract principles and facts but, more importantly, about the people you are fortunate to know.

A NOTE ON NAMES AND DATES

NAMES OF POPES AND BISHOPS IN ARABIC differ from their pronunciation in English. In the first three chapters of the book, English names are used. For example the name of Pope Peter VII (r.* 1809–1852) is used instead of the Arabic Boutros. Starting with Pope Kyrillos IV (r. 1854–1861), the names of popes and bishops are used as they are written in Arabic in order not to confuse the reader who may be familiar with them through other sources.

The exact dates of the reigns of historical popes remain a matter of some debate among scholars. For the purpose of this book, I have relied on the list of dates provided by Otto Meinardus in his book *Two Thousand Years of Coptic Christianity.*

---

* Reigned

CHRONOLOGY

Popes of the Coptic Church		Dynasties and Modern Rulers of Egypt
1. St. Mark	?–68 A.D.	68 A.D. St. Mark is martyred in Alexandria
2. Anianus	68–83	
3. Abilius	83–95	
4. Credon	95–106	
5. Primus	106–118	
6. Justus	118–129	
7. Eumenius	129–141	
8. Marcianus	141–152	
9. Celadion	152–166	
10. Agrippinus	166–178	
11. Julian	178–188	
12. Demetrius I	188–230	
13. Heracles	230–246	
14. Dionysius	246–264	
15. Maximus	264–282	270 St. Anthony the Great goes to the desert
16. Theonas	282–300	284 Emperor Diocletian begins his reign; start of Coptic Calendar
17. Peter I	300–310	
18. Achillas	310–311	
19. Alexander I	311–328	313 Edict of Milan ending persecution issued
		325 1st Ecumenical Council in Nicaea
20. Athanasius I	328–373	
21. Peter II	373–378	
22. Timothy I	378–384	381 2nd Ecumenical Council in Constantinople
23. Theophilus	384–412	
24. Cyril I	412–444	431 3rd Ecumenical Council in Ephesus
25. Dioscorous I	444–454	451 Council of Chalcedon
26. Timothy II	457–477	
27. Peter III	477–489	
28. Athanasius II	489–496	
29. John I	496–505	

30. John II	505–516	
31. Dioscorous II	516–518	
32. Timothy III	518–536	
33. Theodosius I	536–567	
34. Peter IV	567–576	
35. Damian	576–605	
36. Anastasius	605–616	
37. Andronicus	616–623	**619** Persian occupation of Egypt for 10 years
38. Benjamin I	623–662	**641** Egypt falls to army of Amr Ibn El Aas **659** Beginning of Umayyad Caliphate
39. Agathon	662–680	
40. John III	680–689	
41. Isaac	690–692	
42. Simon I	692–700	
43. Alexander II	704–729	**705** Arabic made official language
44. Cosmos I	729–730	
45. Theodore	730–742	
46. Michael I	743–767	**750** Beginning of Abbasid Caliphate
47. Menas I	767–776	
48. John IV	777–799	
49. Mark II	799–819	
50. James	819–830	
51. Simon II	830	
52. Joseph I	831–849	**831** Last Bashmuric revolt
53. Michael II	849–851	
54. Cosmos II	851–858	
55. Shenouda I	859–880	**868** Beginning of Tulunid Dynasty
56. Michael III	880–907	**905** Abbasid Caliphate regains control of Egypt
57. Gabriel I	910–920	
58. Cosmos III	920–932	
59. Macarius I	932–952	**935** Beginning of Ikhshidid Dynasty
60. Theophanes	952–956	
61. Menas II	956–974	**969** Beginning of Fatimid Caliphate
62. Abraham	975–978	
63. Philotheus	979–1003	
64. Zacharias	1004–1032	**1004** Al Hakim begins his persecution of Copts
65. Shenouda II	1032–1046	
66. Christodolos	1047–1077	Seat of papacy moved from Alexandria to Cairo
67. Cyril II	1078–1092	
68. Michael IV	1092–1102	
69. Macarius II	1102–1128	

70. Gabriel II	**1131–1145**	Pope orders liturgy readings to be read in Arabic
71. Michael V	**1145–1146**	
72. John V	**1147–1166**	
73. Mark III	**1166–1189**	**1171** Beginning of Ayyubid Sultanate
74. John VI	**1189–1216**	
75. Cyril III	**1235–1243**	
76. Athanasius III	**1250–1261**	**1252** Beginning of Mamuluk Sultanate
77. John VII	**1262–1268**	
	1271–1293	
78. Gabriel III	**1268–1271**	
79. Theodosius II	**1294–1300**	
80. John VIII	**1300–1320**	
81. John IX	**1320–1327**	
82. Benjamin II	**1327–1339**	
83. Peter V	**1340–1348**	
84. Mark IV	**1348–1363**	
85. John X	**1363–1369**	
86. Gabriel IV	**1370–1378**	
87. Matthew I	**1378–1408**	
88. Gabriel V	**1409–1427**	
89. John XI	**1427–1452**	
90. Matthew II	**1452–1465**	
91. Gabriel VI	**1466–1474**	
92. Michael VI	**1477–1478**	
93. John XII	**1480–1483**	
94. John XIII	**1484–1524**	**1517** Beginning of Ottoman rule in Egypt
95. Gabriel VII	**1525–1570**	
96. John XIV	**1571–1586**	
97. Gabriel VIII	**1587–1603**	
98. Mark V	**1603–1619**	
99. John XV	**1619–1629**	
100. Matthew III	**1631–1646**	
101. Mark VI	**1646–1656**	
102. Matthew IV	**1660–1675**	
103. John XVI	**1676–1718**	
104. Peter VI	**1718–1726**	
105. John XVII	**1727–1745**	
106. Mark VII	**1745–1769**	
107. John XVIII	**1769–1796**	
108. Mark VIII	**1796–1809**	**1798** French invasion
		1805 Mohamed Ali becomes governor of Egypt
109. Peter VII	**1809–1852**	**1817** Dress code imposed for the last time
110. Kyrillos (Cyril) IV	**1854–1861**	**1854** Said Pasha becomes governor

		November 1854 Suez Canal concession
		December 1855 *jizya* abolished
		February 18, 1856 Khat El Hamayuni issued
111. Demetrius II	**1861–1870**	**1863** Khedive Ismail becomes governor
		1866 1st Egyptian parliament meets
112. Kyrillos (Cyril) V	**1874–1927**	**1871** Private property land law issued
		1874 Milli Council established
		1875 Ismail sells shares in Suez Canal to Britain
		1879 Khedive Ismail deposed
		1882 British invasion of Egypt
		1892 Abbas Helmi ascends to the throne
		September 1, 1892 Pope Kyrillos V deposed
		November 29, 1893 Coptic Theological Seminary established
		1906 Aqaba incident
		November 12, 1908 Boutros Ghali becomes first Coptic prime minister
		March 6, 1911 Coptic Conference convenes
		1919 Revolution
		April 1923 Egyptian constitution issued
113. Youannes (John) XIX	**1928–1942**	**1928** Muslim Brotherhood established
114. Macarius III	**1942–1945**	
115. Yusab (Joseph) II	**1946–1956**	**1948** First two of Sunday School Movement become monks
		1952 Free Officers stage coup
		1954 Nasser becomes sole ruler
		1954 Coptic Church joins World Council of Churches
116. Kyrillos (Cyril) VI	**1959–1971**	**September 30, 1962** First two general bishops consecrated
		1964 First priest consecrated for Copts in the West
		1968 Part of relics of St. Mark return to Egypt
		1970 Sadat becomes President
117. Shenouda III	**1971–2012**	**May 1973** Joint Christological Declaration between Coptic and Catholic churches
		December 16, 1976 Coptic Conference
		1976 Missionary work in Africa starts
		September 5, 1981 Sadat removes Pope Shenouda from office and banishes him
		October 6, 1981 Sadat assassinated
		January 25, 2011 Egyptian revolution
118. Tawadros (Theodoros) II	**2012–**	

Motherland Lost

The Egyptian and
Coptic Quest for Modernity

INTRODUCTION

THE TITLE "MOTHERLAND LOST" is not only likely to elicit a sense of gloominess, but might also lead to a misconstrued conception of what this book is about. It is thus appropriate and indeed necessary to start by explaining what this book is not about, before discussing what it is about.

This is not a book about persecution. While the book does indeed cover various aspects of the persecution of Copts in Egypt, it neither aims nor claims to provide an all-encompassing coverage of that distressing story. Readers of this book may be forewarned that they will not find within its pages a listing of each and every attack on Copts or a detailed account of the rampant discrimination they endure.

Nor is this book a history book per se. While it does indeed attempt to cover the long history of the Coptic Orthodox Church of Alexandria and its people, it does not claim to offer a thorough examination of that history. I do not allege to have provided answers to any of the disputable historical incidents and lingering questions. The approach undertaken has not been to solve historical mysteries nor examine their accuracy. Rather, the book approaches those questions with a focus on their modern interpretation, i.e., how they are understood by the various forces and groups in Egypt today. To cite some relevant examples, the book does not aim to prove whether Amr Ibn El Aas burned the Library of Alexandria or whether it is Pope Theophilus who is to be held accountable for such destruction. It is sufficient for the purpose of this book to note how the competing narratives of this incident shape the modern self-perception of Copts. Similarly the book does not claim to determine how many Coptic martyrs died at the hands of Emperor Diocletian or whether the Mokattam Mountain was miraculously moved. It is adequate for the intention of this book to address how those past events are remembered and how they solidified the Coptic Church's identity.

The book engages and refutes two dominating narratives that have shaped the understanding of the Coptic predicament. The first is that of eternal persecution. The story of the plight of modern Copts in Egypt is read as a continuation of their endless suffering whether under Roman and Byzantine emperors or under the rule of Islam. Within this narrative no distinction is made between the diverse forms of persecution that Copts suffered, and the complexity of the modern Coptic problem is obscured.

The second narrative is that of the National Unity discourse. It claims an eternal bond between Copts and Muslims in Egypt, an unbreakable bond that has withstood the test of time. Forever united against foreign intervention, the two "elements" of the Egyptian nation lived in perfect harmony throughout the centuries. Problems, when they are acknowledged, are only temporary and are attributed to the incitement of foreign powers aiming to divide Egyptians or to an invasion of radical views; most notably Wahabisim imported from the Persian Gulf in the '70s. Nasserists, named after their idolized hero Gamal Abdel Nasser, lament the collapse of the nationalist project and blame this collapse for the instigation of the sectarian problem, while liberals nostalgically refer to an idealized Liberal Age in which Christians and Muslims lived together in perfect concord. As will become apparent in later chapters, the reality of Egypt's Liberal Age was quite far from its romanticized version. This book will argue that it is precisely that Liberal Age and the answers developed by its intellectuals to the crisis of modernity that gave birth to the modern Coptic problem.

This book aims to bridge the gap between two different groups of studies. On the one hand, there are excellent works that tackle the Egyptian crisis of modernity. In those works, however, Copts are simply assigned the position of secondary actors who are affected by the overall framework and picture but do not possess any independent agency of their own. Copts seem a minute detail in the overall story, whose fate is simply decided by their fellow countrymen. The Coptic Church as an institution and its own crisis of modernity is ignored. With the exception of a few Coptic intellectuals, e.g., Salama Moussa and Lewis Awad, and a number of politicians, e.g., Makram Ebeid and Boutros Ghali, Copts have been given only limited attention.

On the other hand, there are also excellent historical studies of Coptic issues and history. Nevertheless, these works have, for the most part, ignored completely the overall picture of Egypt at the time they cover. Copts under this approach are dealt with as if they live in a remote island and are discussed as a community that is separated from the rest of society and only marginally affected by events in the country in which they live.

This book aims to tie these two stories together. It will attempt to provide its readers with a clear understanding of who the Copts are, and how the crisis of modernity affected them and their church in conjunction with the overall developments in an Egypt facing its own struggles with modernity. Linking both the Egyptian and Coptic stories, the book argues that the modern plight of Copts is inseparable from the crisis of modernity and the answers developed to address that crisis by the Egyptian state and intellectuals as well as the Coptic Church and laymen. The pace of change that Egypt and the Coptic Church have undergone has not always been the same. Sometimes the church danced to a faster tune, sometimes it was the state that leaped further ahead, but the challenge of modernity remained essentially the same.

With the shock of the discovery of Western technological, material, and military superiority, Egyptians—initially their political rulers but later on intellectuals and the overall population as well—were faced with a crisis that shook the very foundations of their political order. The various answers developed gave rise to the modern political ideologies and movements that exist today.

The initial approach of simply focusing on the importation of Western technology proved inadequate as the gap between Egypt and the West grew only wider. Later on, the West was not simply regarded as a superior other or a model for modernization to be followed, but as a colonizing power as well. As a result the question evolved from "How to catch up?" to, as Bernard Lewis accurately framed it, "What went wrong?" The question had both intellectual and political ramifications.

The book argues that the answers developed by Egyptian intellectuals and by state modernizers to the challenge that modernity posed eventually revolved around the problem of Islam. How to interpret and deal with the apparent contradiction between Islam and modernity has been the key question. It is only with an understanding of how some intellectuals viewed Islam as the problem that one can grasp the meaning of the Muslim Brotherhood's slogan: Islam is the solution.

While affected like their fellow countrymen by this challenge of modernity, Copts were faced with a separate crisis: a specific challenge pertaining to their ancient church and the need for a new orientation and revival in order to be able to deal with modernity and its discontents. The onslaught of foreign missionaries, the challenge of reforming an ancient institution, the impact of the modernizing state, and the clash between the clergy and the laymen were hallmarks of that modern crisis. The laymen's rise to prominence in the state's service and their attempts to answer the overall Egyptian question in turn shaped their approach to the church. The struggles of modernization were fought internally among traditionalists and reformists, but eventually a third current, revivalists, grew and was successful in taking control of the church and shaping that institution and Coptic identity.

The specifically Egyptian crisis of modernity, understood as a question of the compatibility of Islam with modernity, has resulted in the development of various state and intellectual approaches that have shaped the way Copts were viewed and led to their banishment from the public sphere as a community, though not as individuals. The failure of liberalism in Egypt did not result in the Copt's current predicament. Rather, it was the very approach that liberalism took that brought about this predicament.

CHAPTER ONE

Sons of St. Mark

An Altar to the Lord

I
T WAS HIS FIRST DAY IN ALEXANDRIA. He spent the day
walking around the city bedazzled by its wonders. The small
village site that Alexander the Great had chosen to build a city
bearing his name had grown to equal Rome in its greatness. The
largest city in the world, center of the Hellenic dream of the young
conqueror, also housed the largest Jewish community. The city's
library was unmatched with the largest collection of books in the
world, and so were the great temples. Serapis, the ultimate symbol
of the amalgam of Egyptian and Greek mythology, was the city's
protector

He walked for the whole day hardly noticing his hunger and
tiredness. By night the strap of his sandal fell off. He stopped at
the first shoemaker. While repairing the sandal, the shoemaker
accidentally pierced his finger. "*Heis ho Theos* (God is one)" Anianus,
the shoemaker, screamed. The traveller took some mud from the
ground, put it on the wound, and miraculously healed Anianus's
hand. He began telling him how Jesus had died on the cross for
mankind's sins and preached to him the message of Christ. The
message fell on a welcoming heart. Anianus took him to his home
and, with the rest of his family, converted. The visitor baptized
them and in due time ordained Anianus bishop over the city.

9

Thus began the story of Christianity in Egypt. The man who arrived that day was St. Mark, one of the seventy disciples of Christ, according to tradition, and the author of the Gospel bearing his name, but Egypt and its people were no aliens to the biblical storyline. The patriarch Abraham had visited the land of the pharaohs for a short period seeking an escape from a famine in the Holy Land. A longer famine drove Jacob and his sons to Egypt where they were initially protected by Joseph's position, but then for their long enslavement. Even after their escape and return to the Promised Land, Egypt and Babylon remained the main antagonists and quintessential others of the Old Testament.

At the time of the first destruction of the temple and the beginning of the Babylonian captivity, a group of Jews escaped to Egypt, taking with them the prophet Jeremiah. Over the next centuries, these and other Jewish immigrants built a large Jewish community in Egypt. During his reign, Ptolemy II Philadelphus, seeking to complete his growing library, ordered the Jewish scriptures to be translated from Hebrew into Greek. This version, known as the Septuagint in reference to the seventy-two Jewish elders brought in from Israel to do the translation became the accepted text by the church.

But most important to the story, the Lord himself had come to Egypt riding on a swift cloud (the Virgin Mary according to Christian interpretation) as Isaiah 19:1 had prophesied. Joseph had been warned by the angel Gabriel that Herod sought to kill the child, and fled to Egypt with his family. According to later Coptic tradition, the Lord remained in Egypt for three-and-a-half years, travelling throughout the country and blessing it. Hosea had prophesied, "Out of Egypt I called my Son" (Hosea 11:1). This story later on became the center of the Copts' pride. "Blessed be Egypt my people" (Isaiah 19:25). No other people outside of Israel could claim such a connection and take pride in such a blessing.

Copts view themselves as the bearers of this tradition, both the inheritors of the greatness of the pharaohs and the heroes of Christianity. If some historical events are deemed still relevant in the Middle East, for Copts this is not ancient history, it is who they are.

Egypt at the time was under the rule of the Roman Empire and was its most prosperous province, the breadbasket that fed Rome. Cleopatra had conquered the hearts of Julius Caesar and Mark Antony, and Augustus made Egypt part of his empire in the year 31 BC after the battle of Actium. The cities were Hellenized and Greek was the language of culture, but the countryside remained as Egyptian as it ever was. There the Egyptian language reached its final development in the Coptic language. Coptic was the last stage of the Egyptian language; it was written using the Greek alphabet and borrowing seven signs from the Demotic script to cover sounds not available in Greek.

Unlike in other parts of the Roman Empire, Christianity does not seem to have spread initially among Jews only, but more so among Egypt's native population. It remains an open question as to why Egyptians adopted the new religion with such speed and rose to defend it with such vigor offering themselves as martyrs for their newly acquired faith. Some attribute it to a closeness of the idea of the Trinity to ancient Egyptian mythology, others to an early form of native nationalism, but for Copts the answer was quite simple; the heart of Egypt had been touched by the Lord and they became his people. "So the Lord will make himself known to the Egyptians, and in that day they will acknowledge the Lord. They will worship with sacrifices and grain offerings; they will make vows to the Lord and keep them" (Isaiah 19:21).

One chapter remains before the story of Jesus and Egypt is concluded for Copts. According to Coptic tradition, after his resurrection, the Lord took the Virgin Mary and his disciples to Mount Koskam in the south of Egypt, a place he had visited with

Mary and Joseph as a child, and there he conducted the first Mass. This site is today the Monastery of the Virgin Mary (*Al Muhharaq*) and there remains the altar believed to have been used by the Lord. Isaiah had after all prophesied, "In that day there will be an altar to the Lord in the heart of Egypt, and a monument to the Lord at its border" (Isaiah 19:19).

With their newly found passion for Christianity, Egyptians joined the new religion in droves. Fragments from the second century indicate a growing and thriving community. St. Mark returned to Alexandria and shed his blood there in the year 68 AD Martyrdom would become associated with the Church of Alexandria more than with any other early Christian church, and would become a cornerstone of its identity. Anianus followed St. Mark on the papal seat. The chain continues to today with the selection of Pope Tawadros II as the 118th pope of Alexandria in 2012.

But St. Mark did not only give Egyptians his gospel and blood, he also gave them a cornerstone of their new faith: the Catechetical School of Alexandria. According to Coptic tradition, he established the school and appointed Justus as its first manager. Whether the story is true or whether the establishment of the school is a later development, it is no surprise that such a school would emerge in Alexandria. Alexandria was home to the greatest philosophers and pagan thinkers of the time. If Christianity was to succeed in finding a place for itself there, it had to be able to compete with Greek philosophy and defeat it.

The school's fame spread across the world of late antiquity. Its early deans included such distinguished philosophers and theologians as Pantaenus (died 200), Clement of Alexandria (150–215) and the greatest thinker of the early church, Origen (184–254). The school would continue to flourish well into the fourth century under the leadership of Didymus the Blind (313–398) who, fifteen centuries before Braille, invented a system for the blind to read. As the most outstanding theological school in the Christian world, it played a significant role initially in the field of Christian apologetic and later sought to reconcile Greek philosophy with Christianity. Later on, it became the most important Christian theological school in fighting heretics from the Gnostics to Arius. Western theologians such as St. Jerome would travel to Alexandria to drink from its fountain of wisdom.

The school, however, was not without its own controversies. Some of Clement's works were frowned upon by later theologians, but it was Origen who caused the greatest controversy. Perhaps the greatest theologian in the history of Christianity, Origen had both devoted admirers and many detractors among the fathers of the early church. His works were praised by such men as St. Athanasius and St. John Chrysostom while condemned by Pope Theophilus of Alexandria and Epiphanius of Salamis. His numerous works, his conflict with and condemnation by Pope Demetrius of Alexandria (r.* 188–230), and his self-castration in a literal interpretation of Matthew 19:12 would become the center of debates within the universal church for centuries after his death.

Heresies and theological differences were a mark of the early church. Gnosticism was the greatest challenge of the second and third centuries and it was no surprise that it would find a receptive audience among Egyptian Christians. Egyptian Gnostics would leave the world one of the greatest treasures of ancient writings in the documents that were discovered in Nag Hammadi in 1945. That treasure included fifty-two apocryphal texts rejected by the early church fathers such as the Gospel of Thomas, the Gospel of Truth, and the Gospel of Philip. These works have not only given modern scholars an incredible insight into the early church but

---

* Reigned.

have also helped ignite modern controversies and conspiracy theories such as that of *The Da Vinci Code*.

Martyrdom was a central theme of the first church, but nowhere was it to become the hallmark of its identity as in Egypt. It is difficult to overstate the importance of martyrdom to the Coptic Church both in its early years and until today as a pillar of how the church views itself. For the Coptic Church and its people, persecution and martyrdom were the founding theme of their history and identity whether under the Romans, Byzantines, or under the rule of Islam. Jesus had warned his disciples that, "A servant is not greater than his master. If they persecuted me, they will persecute you also." (John 15:20.) The martyrdom of St. Mark in 68 AD was soon followed by rivers of Egyptian blood.

The first wave of persecution took place under the Roman Emperor Nero, but for the Coptic Church its real beginning was under the reign of Domitian (81–96). A few years of relative quiet were always followed by a new wave of persecution, often stronger than the previous one, under the reigns of Emperors Trajan (98–117), Hadrian (117–138), Marcus Aurelius (161–180), Septimus Severus (193–211), Maximus Thrax (235–238), Decius (249–251), and Valerian (253–260). At times, persecution was instigated by local unrest and mob violence, at others it was government organized and hence more systematic and widespread.

No persecution, however, compared to that which the Emperor Diocletian (284–305) unleashed. In Coptic tradition, his reign is called the "Era of the Martyrs." Though his persecution of Christians began in 303, it was so severe that Copts marked the first year of his accession to the throne as the beginning of their own calendar. While some modern historians have de-emphasized the brutality and scope of the persecution, arguing that all in all only around 3,000 Christians were killed throughout the empire, according to Coptic historical texts tens of thousands of

Copts were murdered for refusing to sacrifice to Roman gods. Chief among these were the Coptic Pope Peter of Alexandria (r. 300–310), St. Menas (285–309), St. Demiana and the Theban Legion.* Though a non-Egyptian, St. George who was martyred at the time, would later become perhaps the most important saint in the Coptic Church.

The narrative of the persecuted church, the theme of Egypt as the land that paid an unparalleled price for its faith in Christ, would become central to the Copt's self-understanding. Generations would be told of the heavy price in blood that their ancestors paid for them to receive this faith, whether at the hands of the Romans, or later on at the hands of their fellow co-religionists the Byzantine emperors, or at the hands of Muslims. While the narrative of the endless persecution would lead to acceptance of discrimination and persecution as a necessary and natural aspect of their faith, it would also give Copts great pride and internal strength. If all those emperors, caliphs, kings, and rulers could not break the Coptic Church, no one could.

The Church Triumphant

The Edict of Milan issued by Constantine the Great and his co-Emperor Licinius in 313 finally ended the persecution of Christians. The celebration was however short-lived. If Roman persecution had bloodied Christianity and threatened its existence, the church was soon to learn that peace was sometimes more threatening than war. Heresies, while not new phenomena, were soon to take a more dramatic turn, tearing the church apart.

---

* A Roman legion originally garrisoned in the Egyptian city of Thebes which was martyred in Switzerland.

Egypt was not only a major battlefield of that fight but provided the main antagonists on both sides.

Arius (250–336) was of Libyan descent but his career and controversy started in Egypt. His argument was quite simple, the Trinity was not equal. Jesus, the Son, was not equal to the Father. Based on his reading and interpretation of such Biblical passages as, "For the Father is greater than I" (John 14:28), he concluded that the Son was inferior to the Father and that there was a point in time when the Son did not exist, was thus created, and was not similar to the Father in substance. He first made his views known at the time of Pope Peter of Alexandria, the seventeenth of the Coptic popes, who excommunicated him. He was later readmitted to the church by Peter's successor Achillas (r. 310–311). The real controversy, however, started under the following pope, Alexander (r. 311–328). Pope Alexander had given a sermon preaching the equality of the Trinity which Arius condemned as heresy. The conflict soon spread beyond the city of Alexandria, with bishops and priests throughout the country taking sides. Threatened by the possibility of a real schism, Alexander first called a local synod in Alexandria in 320 and then a national one in 321 in which Arius and his views were condemned.

But if Alexander thought this would end the matter, his hopes were soon crushed. The fires ignited by Arius had already spread outside Egypt. Arius had gained the support of some bishops in Greater Syria and modern Turkey, most important of whom was Eusebius of Nicomedia who had the emperor's ear. The church was being torn apart and a solution had to be found. A plea by the emperor himself to end the controversy fell on deaf ears. Constantine, seeking a final solution, took the unprecedented move in 325 of calling for an ecumenical council to be held in Nicaea. Every bishop in the Roman Empire was invited, 318 are said to have attended. The council would become a landmark event in church history and the first of many to come.

But it was none of those gathering bishops who was to emerge as the star of the council, nor was it Alexander or Arius, but another Egyptian: Athanasius. Athanasius, whose name is often followed by "The Great" or, in Coptic tradition, "The Apostolic," would dominate the world of Christendom for the following fifty years. At the time of Nicaea, Athanasius was a twenty-seven-year-old deacon. He attended the gathering as Pope Alexander's personal secretary. According to Coptic tradition, Pope Alexander had first noticed Athanasius, when looking from his window; he had seen him leading a group of children mimicking the process of baptism. Playing the role of bishop, Athanasius perfectly imitated the rituals impressing the pope who, after questioning him, decided to take him as his student. The young man's talents soon became quite obvious. He mastered not only Christian theology but also pagan philosophy at the Alexandrian School.

According to Coptic tradition, it was Athanasius who challenged Arius at Nicaea and proved his arguments heretic. He was tasked with writing the Creed of faith that would become known as the Nicene Creed and that to this day is recognized nearly unanimously among Christians. The famous lines "the only begotten Son of God, begotten by the Father before all worlds," and "begotten not made, being of one substance with the Father" would become the foundation of what the very word Christian entails. The council was also important for its decisions on the baptism of heretics, the Meletian schism, and the exact date of the celebration of Easter, separating it from the Jewish calendar and thus endorsing the position of Alexandria and Rome against that of Eastern churches. It would also prove important in the future conflict between Alexandria and Rome over the papacy's powers as the Sixth Canon of Nicaea stressed the supreme authority that

Alexandria, Antioch, and Rome each had in their respective territories. Most importantly, Nicaea would become significant for the precedent it created with the Emperor Constantine presiding over the council and confirming its rulings. The affairs of the church would no longer be its business alone as successive emperors sought, and were in many cases successful, to control the councils, choosing sides among the fighting bishops and in some cases deciding what Christian faith entailed.

If the bishops who gathered in Nicaea hoped that their council would end the Arian controversy, they were quickly proven wrong. Arianism would continue to tear the heart of Christianity apart for the next fifty years. While the church celebrates many saints who fought Arianism for those fifty years such as St. Basil the Great, Saint Gregory the Theologian, and Saint Hilary of Poitiers, all considered Pillars of the Church, the fate of the Nicene Creed depended upon the vigor and conviction of one man: Athanasius the Great.

In 328, three years after Nicaea, Pope Alexander died. Athanasius was the natural successor though some objections were raised due to his young age, reportedly less than thirty. His first years as the pope of Alexandria were unremarkable and he spent them visiting his vast diocese, but those years of tranquility were only the quiet before the storm. By 335, his Arian enemies won the emperor's favor and gathered enough strength to hold a council at Tyre and throw a series of accusations at Athanasius, who managed to clear his name. One accusation however, that of threatening to cut the grain supply to the capital, was sufficient for the emperor to order him exiled to Germany. Athanasius remained there until Constantine's death. It would be only the first of five exiles during which he would be forced to escape the wrath of his enemies and emperors.

The importance of Athanasius in the Coptic Church's view of itself cannot be overstated. During his exiles in Europe, he would publish his biography of St. Anthony the Great and help bring monasticism to the West. Defender of the faith, hero of Christianity, banished, assaulted, cursed, forced into hiding, but never relenting, the rock on which Arianism was crushed. His life can be summoned in a conversation with a friend who warned him that everyone was against him, the bishops, priests and the emperor himself. "The whole world is against you Athanasius," the friend said, to which Athanasius replied: "*Athanasius Contra Mundum*," I am against the world.

The Salt of the Earth

If martyrdom and the Catechetical School of Alexandria, with its heroes defining and defending the true faith, were the two pillars of the Coptic Church and its definition of itself, the third pillar was monasticism. It was perhaps the greatest contribution of the Coptic Church to Christianity. The light of Coptic monks such as St. Anthony the Great (251–356), St. Macarius, Lamp of the Desert (died 395), and St. Pachomius the Great (292–348) shined throughout the world and their piousness, humility, and miraculous lives set the example for millions to follow. The Desert Fathers, Planets of the Wilderness—the wisdom of these simple men was sought by emperors, and their poor cells in the desert became pilgrimage sites for Christians throughout the empire, some of whom would stay and become their disciples.

The idea of living in solitude in the desert for a period of time in order to reflect and pray was certainly not a new phenomenon. The Old Testament is rich with examples such as Moses and Elijah. John the Baptist's life also provided a model and so did the forty days Jesus spent in the wilderness before his temptation. The Apostle Paul mentions a time he spent in Arabia in his letter to

the Galatians. Those sojourns were brief, however, and did not
involve any organization. It was with St. Anthony the Great that
monasticism would begin.

The call for monasticism came from an interpretation of famous
Biblical passages such as Matthew 19:21: "If you want to be perfect, go, sell what you have and give to the poor, and you will have
treasure in heaven; and come, follow Me." And Matthew 19:12:
"For there are some eunuchs, which were so born from their
mother's womb: and there are some eunuchs, which were made
eunuchs of men: and there be eunuchs, which have made themselves eunuchs for the kingdom of heaven's sake. He that is able to
receive it let him receive it." The first passage was the call for poverty, while the second was read as a call to celibacy. The third pillar
of monasticism, obedience, would be developed along the way.

St. Anthony the Great was certainly not the first hermit living
in the desert. He himself learned that lesson when, tempted by the
Devil to think of himself as such, he was instructed in a vision to
seek the first hermit, Paul of Thebes. But while not the first monk,
he is credited with creating Christian monasticism due to the disciples soon gathering around him and the example he set for others to follow. He sought complete solitude deep in the Egyptian
Eastern Desert. If he hoped to escape people, his hopes were soon
crushed as his fame soon attracted disciples who flocked to follow
him. Among them was St. Macarius who would become the Father
of those monks living in Sketis. Nitria, Kellia, and Sketis would
soon house thousands of monks living in extremely harsh conditions and dividing their time between prayers and handwork
mostly weaving cloth and baskets.

Monasticism in the Egyptian deserts took three forms. First
there were those monks such as St. Karas who lived totally
secluded often for decades without any interaction with human
beings. The second form was more organized and had its tradi-

tion in the community that emerged around St. Macarius. Monks would live in separate cells and caves but gather for the Divine Liturgy or for spiritual guidance. Those monks would be living under the guidance of a renowned monk who was experienced in the life of the desert. As some found the totally secluded life hard to follow, St. Pachomius developed a third form called cenobitic monasticism which gathered disciples into monasteries. Monks would live together in one or more building and share a life of prayers and work. This system was copied by St. Basil the Great in the East and formed the model that St. Benedict would use in the West.

The reputation of those Coptic monks and their example would in time lead many foreigners to travel to the Egyptian deserts to join them. St. Arsanius the Great (350–445) left a life as an imperial tutor while St. Moses the Black (330–405) abandoned his life as a thief to become Stars of the Egyptian Desert, as the most famous monks were called. The lives of those monks and their sayings would be recorded by Palladius in his Lausiac History and in the *"Apophthegmata Patrum"* (Sayings of the Desert Fathers). Many of the pilgrims who came to the Egyptian desert would later start monastic communities in their own countries.

Coptic monasticism was not a way of life chosen solely by men. Coptic tradition holds that St. Anthony the Great left his sister with Christian virgins who were living together. Later on, female monasteries sprang up all around Egypt. These monasteries often were not in the desert proper but much closer to the Nile. They were often attached or in close proximity to male monasteries, both for receiving communion and for protection. There were, however, also female hermits who lived a life of complete desert solitude such as St. Mary of Egypt (344–421). Coptic tradition also identifies a number of female saints who lived among the hermits disguised as men such as St. Theodora of Alexandria.

Monasticism is crucial in understanding the Coptic Church and its self-identity. The attempt to live the lives of angels in the deserts of Egypt would create an identification of virtue with that desert life to the determent of secular life. Monks would thus become the most important category in the church at the expense of both the priests and the rest of the general population as through the centuries piety became definable only in monastic terms. A tradition soon emerged whereby only monks could be chosen as bishops and popes further entrenching their control of the church. The rise of monasticism would also lead inevitably to the collapse of the Catechetical School. If the simple life was what was needed to enter heaven, what was the need for philosophy and knowledge? While the Coptic Church would continue throughout the centuries to offer renowned theologians, they would be small in number. The monastic emphasis on obedience would also leave its imprint on the Coptic Church's attitude and teachings. St. John the Dwarf is said to have been given a stick by his teacher St. Pambo and ordered to plant it and water it. St. John complied and watered it for three years twice a day, even though the water was twelve miles away from where they lived. After those three years, the stick grew into a fruitful tree. St. Pambo took its fruits and sent it to the fathers of the desert saying: "Take, eat from the fruit of obedience." The tree survived until quite recently at the site of the deserted Monastery of Saint John the Dwarf in the Nitrian Desert, when a Bedouin cut it down. This story is at the center of the Coptic Church's teaching and regardless of its truthfulness set the model for its people to follow.

The Church Torn Apart

Arianism's final defeat at the second Ecumenical Council in Constantinople in 381 hardly brought peace and tranquility to the church. It proved to be only the beginning of a long set of heresies, struggles, and disputes that tore the church apart. A small controversy over the divinity of the Holy Spirit would soon give way to a larger one on the nature of the Son. Origen's writings still ignited fierce debates and were soon at the center of angry disputes in the Egyptian deserts[1] which quickly spilled over to Constantinople, where its archbishop, St. John Chrysostom, found himself the target of the wrath of Egypt's Pope Theophilus (r. 384–412) and was eventually condemned and banished.[2] Theological disputes got tied to political struggles with the emperors heavily involved in deciding the soundness of doctrines. The churches found themselves in a deadly competition where the struggle over honor, position, and power proved to be as important as the fight over what constituted the true Christian faith. Simultaneously Alexandria's popes were busy eradicating paganism, often using violent methods.[3]

Trouble soon erupted again in Constantinople where its archbishop, Nestorius, was adamant on calling the Virgin Mary "Christotokos," Mother of Christ, instead of "Theotokos,"

---

1. The fight was over the question of whether those passages in the scripture that described God's face or hands were to be understood literally or metaphorically. At the time, most of the monks in the Egyptian deserts held an anthropomorphic simple view of God in stark contrast to those, following the teachings of Origen, who held an incorporeal view of God.

2. Pope Theophilus's conduct from the start of the controversy left a lot to be desired. His treatment of St. John Chrysostom, who is now considered a Father of the Church, was however the most damaging to his reputation. Theophilus remains a controversial figure to the present day and while the Coptic Church considers him a saint, his name is significantly absent from the absolution of the liturgy.

3. The burning of the Serapeum in 391 at the hands of Pope Theophilus and the murder of the philosopher Hypatia in 415 and the exact role Pope Cyril played in that murder continues to be a matter of scholarly and public debate.

Mother of God.[4] News of his views was received with horror in
Alexandria, where its pope, Cyril I (r. 412–444) who would later
be called Pillar of the Faith, condemned them. An ecumenical
council soon convened in Ephesus in 431, the third such council
in church history and the last one recognized by the Coptic
Church. When Nestorius refused to back down, he was excommunicated. Cyril's proclamation on the unity of the divine and
human natures in Christ as "a union without any division, change,
or confusion" was declared the correct Orthodox belief. The council proclaimed that Jesus was one person, complete God and complete man, perfect in his divinity and perfect in his humanity.

The flames of the Nestorian heresy had barely died out before
they were lit once again in Constantinople. If Nestorius swung the
pendulum in one direction, Eutyches swung it in the other by
preaching that Christ's divinity had consumed his humanity as an
ocean consumes a drop of water. Pope Dioscorous (r. 444–454)
decided to get involved. A council he chaired ended up absolving
Eutyches from any guilt and excommunicating his detractors.
Pope Leo of Rome was appalled. Many bishops later claimed that
they were threatened into agreeing with Dioscorous. If Alexandria
had managed to strike at its competitors in the council, their revenge
was not long in waiting.

Two years later the tables had completely turned. The new
emperor, Marcian, ordered another council convened, this time at
Chalcedon in 451, and Dioscorous found himself in the position of
the accused. In theological terms, the two sides are today understood as not as far apart as they seemed to the participants in those

---

4. The difference was not over a simple title but was rooted in Nestorius's
belief that a union between God and man was impossible and thus that
Christ was essentially two separate persons in one body.

debates, with the gap being less of a theological difference than one of terminology with different understandings of the word "nature" in Latin and Greek. Both sides agreed that a union had taken place between the two natures and while Leo, the pope of Rome, stressed that Christ had two natures that are together in one hypostasis, his Alexandrian counterpart stressed that the union had resulted in "one nature of God, the Word Incarnate." The thin line between both positions rests in whether Christ is "from two natures" as Dioscorous stressed or "in two natures" as Leo believed.[5] The political struggle between the churches over supremacy was at the heart of what took place in Chalcedon, but it found its expression in theological differences. The council ended with Dioscorous and his Egyptian bishops banished from their seats. The council appointed a new patriarch for Alexandria, Proterius.

The news of Dioscorous's banishment and the appointment of Proterius were met with rejection by the majority of Egypt's Christians who refused to follow the new patriarch and remained loyal to Dioscorous. For them, Dioscorous was a hero of the Orthodox faith and they resented attempts by Byzantine emperors and Roman popes to interfere in their religious affairs, dictate the faith they were to follow, and choose their leaders. The theological separation gave rise to a linguistic one as well with Coptic increasingly used instead of Greek as the language of the church. Credit for the linguistic shift as well as fierce opposition to Chalcedon and defense of Coptic views lay with Shenouda the Archimandrite (348–466). Monasteries became the center of the Copt's resistance to imperial interference in their church's affairs.

---

5. Those who rejected Chalcedon would be called Monophysites, though the Coptic Church rejects the term and uses the term Miaphysite instead. Chalcedoneans are called Dyophysits.

While attempts would be made at reconciliation such as the Henotikon[6] and some popes would be jointly recognized by what were increasingly two distinct communities of Christians in Egypt, the schism at Chalcedon proved permanent continuing until the present day. Supporters of Chalcedon in Egypt would be called Melkite[7] meaning followers of the emperor. Increasingly the divide took ethnic terms with the Greek minority adhering to the Chalcedonian position while native Egyptians remained loyal to their Coptic church. There were now two different men claiming the seat of St. Mark. However, one of them, the Chalcedonian patriarch resided in Alexandria and was able to exercise his authority, while the other, the Coptic pope, could not exercise power publically and was often in hiding. This pattern would continue until the Arab invasion.

Many of the later trademarks of the Coptic Church were adopted and developed during this period. John I (r. 496–505) would be the first pope to be chosen from among the monks in the Egyptian deserts and not from the clergy in Alexandria, a tradition that has continued with small intervals until today. It was during the papacy of John II (r. 505–516) that the relationship with Antioch and its Syriac Orthodox Church would become unbreakable. The link saw its greatest flourishing under Severus (patriarch of Antioch 512–538) who found refuge in Egypt from the emperor's troops. Until today, Severus's name is read in the Absolution during Coptic Liturgy right after St. Mark's and before those of

6. The Henotikon was a compromise formula adopted by Emperor Zeno. The new policy upheld the condemnation of both Nestorius and Eutyches and endorsed Cyril's Twelve Anathemas as the measure of faith and completely ignored taking any position on the question of the two natures. As a compromise, it managed to bring the Eastern Empire some decades of religious peace though it resulted in a schism with Rome which lasted until 519 when Emperor Justin I reestablished relations with Rome.
7. The word Melkite comes from the Semitic word for king.

such Egyptian fathers as Athanasius, Cyril, and Dioscorous. A tradition of exchanging letters reaffirming commitment to the non-Chalcedonian faith between the two patriarchs continued largely uninterrupted until the present. Those churches together with the Armenian Apostolic Church, the Malankara Orthodox Syrian Church in India, and the Coptic church's daughter churches in Ethiopia and Eritrea form Oriental Orthodoxy, a term aiming to distinguish between them and Eastern Orthodoxy which accepts Chalcedon and is widespread in Russia and Eastern Europe.

The imperial persecution of Copts intensified during the last century of Byzantine rule. Emperors were determined to put an end to the theological differences that were threatening to tear the empire apart. Coptic churches fell in the hands of Melkites who had the backing of the local governors. Byzantine persecution of Copts would leave a lasting impact on Copts, an impact that would be remembered and reinforced during the Crusades. Byzantine persecution ceased for a short interval as a result of the Sassanid Persian occupation of Egypt between 619 and 629. The exhaustive war between the empires would leave them both severely wounded and weak, opening the door to the Arab invasion that would crush both. The brief return to Byzantine rule and attempts to enforce conformity would be recorded as being quite severe and would prove to be the last contact between Copts and the rest of Christianity before the Arab invasion built a wall of separation and entrenched Copts as an isolated community. The fight against Chalcedon and royal interference in the affairs of the Coptic Church would write a new chapter in the story of a church and a people against the world.

CHAPTER TWO

Under the Banner of Islam

THE ARABS AT THE GATES

HARDLY HAD BYZANTINE RULE IN EGYPT settled down after the defeat of the Sassanids than a new threat appeared on the horizon. Arab tribes, united by their new religion, began pouring out of the desert and challenging both the Byzantine and Sassanid Empires. Spectacular victories lay before them. Damascus fell in 634, Jerusalem in 637, and Antioch in the same year. Simultaneously, Muslim armies were conquering Iraq and soon enough Persia itself. With Muslim rule established in Greater Syria, it was natural for them to look toward Egypt.

Indeed, the connection with Egypt was older. According to Muslim tradition, the prophet of Islam, Mohamed, had sent emissaries to the kings of the world. These included the Byzantine emperor, the Sassanid king, the king of Ethiopia, the ruler of Bahrain, the Arab ruler of Syria, and a certain Muqawqis who was ruler of Egypt. While the identity of that Muqawqis would became an issue of heated debate that continues until this day, it is the inclusion of a letter to what was at best a local governor that is quite curious. Al Muqawqis, though not converting, sent Mohamed a gift and two female slaves, one of whom, Maria the Copt, as

Islamic tradition names her, became Mohamed's concubine,[1] and later bore him his son, Ibrahim. It is in this context that a number of Hadiths* attributed to Mohamed are understood: "You will conquer Egypt, a land where the Qirat† is used, Treat its people kindly since they have a right of kinship upon you" and "By Allah, respect Copts of Egypt, for you shall conquer them, and they shall be your supporters in the cause of Allah."

Amr Ibn El Aas, the future conqueror of Egypt is alleged to have visited it earlier as a trader. His admiration for its wealth and grandeur is said to have influenced him greatly, leading him to urge the caliph Omar to invade it. Regardless of the truthfulness of such stories, the fact that an Arab Syria would be threatened by Byzantine forces from both Asia Minor and Egypt meant that a decision to invade Egypt was inevitable. Amr crossed the Egyptian border with four thousand men in 639 and, after receiving some eight thousand men in reinforcements, managed to conquer Babylon in 640. After a siege, Alexandria finally fell in 641. With the fall of Alexandria, no other city could muster a defense to the invading army, and Egypt was fully conquered. Although the Byzantine Empire would retake Alexandria for a short period in 645, the fate of Egypt had already been sealed.

The quick fall of Egypt with minor losses to the invading Arab army would become a puzzle and ignite a contentious debate that continues to modern times. During the height of Egyptian nationalism in the first decades of the twentieth century, propagators of the narrative of national unity between Egypt's Christians and

---

* A saying or act ascribed to the Prophet Mohamed.
† A form of measurement.
1. There is some debate among Islamic scholars whether Maria is considered a wife or merely a concubine. The earliest traditions all agree on her concubine status.

Muslims would employ the successful invasion story as proof that Copts welcomed the Arab Muslim invasion and thus as a cornerstone of the eternal unity of the two communities. The rise of the alternative Islamic identity would stress the story as one of rescue. Islamist writers would play on the theme of a possible end to non-Chalcedonian Christianity in Egypt had it not been for its preservation by the invading Muslim army. For Copts, who have suffered increasing discrimination in recent years, the rejection of both narratives is important to their self-identity and their modern struggle. Modern Coptic authors have stressed that their great-grandfathers did not welcome the invasion. Some of them portrayed general passivity towards both the Byzantines and Arabs, while others have stressed early stories of Coptic resistance to the invasion. One issue that would emerge as significant in modern times is the question of whether Egypt submitted to the Muslims or was conquered by them. Muslim scholars had written extensively about various cities in Egypt and their status in those two categories. The distinction is of vital importance given the later emphasis on and arguments about what peaceful submission by an agreement entails for the *dhimmi** population and their rights.

Related to the question of how welcoming Copts were to the invasion is that of how destructive it was. Modern Muslim scholars have portrayed the invasion as kind to the country's inhabitants and free of any massacres or atrocities. Amr asked the non-Chalcedonian Pope Benjamin I (r. 623–662) to emerge from hiding and treated him well. This image is in contrast to that presented by modern Coptic writers who have highlighted the brutality of the invasion citing Christian sources from the time such

---

* *Dhimmi* is the Islamic term used to describe non-Muslim citizens of the Islamic state. Initially the term was limited to Jews and Christians.

as John of Nikiu as well as early Muslim authors such as Ibn Abd
El Hakam.[2] Tied to that narrative is the controversy over the
burning of the Library of Alexandria. Copts hold Amr responsible
for that act, which is portrayed as a sign of brutality and barbar-
ity due to Bedouin ignorance of the value of knowledge.[3] The
Coptic narrative portrays a cruel Arab invasion both in the massacres committed as well as the conditions they imposed on the
local population. This narrative also highlights later Coptic revolts
against their rulers, rejecting the narrative of Coptic passivity;
some writers draw a line through history of Coptic nationalism
and its eternal struggle against oppression in contrast to descriptions of Copts as largely passive to persecution, past and present.
Accordingly, modern Coptic writers have debated the role of
Coptic popes at the time and whether their acceptance of persecution as a natural fate for Christians in this world played a role
in pacifying their community and helping the Muslim invaders
conquer the country. The church's failure of its people has served
as a theme for some modern writers angry at the perceived passivity of the modern church under Pope Shenouda III during
Mubarak's rule.

---

2. Several modern books by Coptic authors take this line such as Father
Metias Menkarious's *Copts: A Struggle for Survival,* Father Bigol Basily's *Did
Copts Welcome the Arab Conquest?,* and Bishop Youannes of Gharbia's *History
of the Coptic Church after the Council of Chalcedon.* Also taking the same argument is the important study by Sanaa El Masry "Margins of the Arab Conquest of Egypt: Tales of Entry & Journal of Fusion."

3. The question of who burned the Library of Alexandria causing the
great loss to humanity remains unsettled, and has become a topic of heated
debate between Copts and Muslims in modern times. Some cite the destruction of the Serapeum in 391 at the hands of Pope Theophilus as cause for the
fire, while other historical accounts blame Julius Caesar and Aurelian. Based
on accounts by later Muslim historians, Copts place the blame on the shoulders of Amr upon orders of the Caliph Omar.

THE CHURCH AND STATE

The commencement of Muslim rule offered the Coptic Church a brief period of catching its breath. After years of the pope being forced to hide in the face of Byzantine persecution, Pope Benjamin was able to return to Alexandria and begin to rebuild what had been destroyed. This rebuilding effort took various forms: repairing churches and monasteries that were destroyed during the Sassanid invasion, reclaiming churches that the Chalcedonians had overtaken, and consecrating bishops and priests in the many parishes that had lost theirs during the previous years. It also provided an opportunity to deal with minor schisms that had emerged within the church. This period of calm lasted for nearly forty years in which the church was largely left to its own devices by the new rulers.

Both the Umayyad and Abbasid caliphates maintained a policy of repeatedly changing the governor of Egypt. During the Umayyad's ninety-one years in power, twenty-five men occupied the governor's seat. The Abbasids proved to be faster in changing their governors, with seventy-eight men serving as governor during their 118-year rule. This policy, while intended to ensure that no governor would entrench his position and thus become powerful enough to challenge the caliph, proved disastrous for Egypt in general and the Coptic Church in particular. Given that every new governor knew that his days in Egypt were numbered, he had no interest in long-term plans for the province and instead focused on collecting as much money as possible. This meant higher taxation on Copts as well as attempts to extort as much money as possible from their popes.

The first such case involved Pope John III (r. 680–689) who was thrown in prison by Abdel Aziz Ibn Marwan for a perceived insult and forced to pay a sum of money to gain his release. Governor

Abdallah Ibn Abdel Malek arrested Pope Alexander II (r. 704–729) for the purpose of extracting a sum of money from him. In order to pay it, Pope Alexander II was forced to travel throughout Egypt to raise money for the fine imposed on him. This tactic was repeated again in the cases of Pope Michael I (r. 743–767) and Pope Michael III (r. 880–907).

For the Muslim governors of Egypt, the Coptic pope served as a liaison in dealing with the local population. This proved to be a curse for successive popes, who were usually held accountable at any sign of trouble be it a local rebellion or the failure of Copts to pay the required taxation. The Bashmuric revolt thus led to the imprisonment and torture of Pope Michael I at the hands of Marwan II, the last Umayyad caliph.

Governors of Egypt naturally showed an interest in the position of pope and attempted to intervene in the selection process. This interference is first recorded at the time of the selection of Pope Isaac (r. 690–692). Initially it took the form of merely requiring that Copts inform the governor of the death of the previous pope and receive his approval to select another. A difference of opinion between Copts at the time of the selection of Pope Simon I (r. 692–700) led them to bring their disagreement to the governor thus increasing his involvement in the process. This power became manifest when one governor refused to allow Copts to select a new pope, Michael I, and left them waiting until his successor granted the required permission.

In some cases, the caliph in Damascus or Baghdad would order that a Christian friend of his be enthroned in place of the sitting pope. Such interference in church affairs would naturally be faced with rejection by Copts and their clergy who would continue supporting their pope. Pope Agatho (r. 662–680) was the first to undergo this ordeal. This ugly form of intrusion was repeated again during the reign of Pope Mina I (r. 767–776) who was forced to perform hard labor.

The pope's role as the religious leader of the Ethiopian[4] and Nubian churches was another source of problems as he was forced to play a diplomatic role on behalf of the rulers of Egypt. During the first centuries of Muslim rule, Nubia was the more important of the two given its location on Egypt's southern border and that Muslims had largely failed to invade it. Pope Joseph I (r. 831–849) was thus forced to write a letter to the king of Nubia urging him to pay the required *jizya*. As time went by, the Coptic pope's role as diplomat would increase and would also be a reason for suspicion. Muslim rulers would attempt to monitor and control the relationship between the pope and the church in Nubia and Ethiopia. Pope Simon I was accused of consecrating a bishop for India without first informing the governor. Sometimes the rulers of Nubia and Ethiopia would plead or intervene on behalf of the Coptic pope. The king of Nubia is reported to have invaded Egypt when he heard of the mistreatment of Pope Michael I.

Learning Dhimmitude

The need to find ways to navigate their new position under Muslim domination was a task not limited to the church leadership. The rest of the Coptic community was beginning to learn what

---

4. Christianity was brought to Ethiopia in the fourth century by Frumentius, who was later consecrated as bishop of Ethiopia by Pope Athanasius. Ever since, an Egyptian monk has always been chosen for the post and the Ethiopian church continued following its Coptic mother church for over sixteen hundred years. Today, while separate, both churches share the same tenets of faith.

their new status meant. In the early years of Muslim rule, the question of occupying high-ranking government jobs and the need for physical distinction emerges only in minor incidents. Naturally, given that the population of Egypt was Christian and that initially very few Arabs came to live there, the question of employing Copts in government service was answered in the affirmative. The new rulers could not afford, even if they so desired, a complete overhaul of the bureaucracy; whatever misgivings they held regarding employing non-believers had to wait for the future. Similarly given the limited number of Muslim Arabs in the country and the lack of a huge pool of converts from the local population, the need for distinction in terms of clothes and habits did not emerge. The invaders and the local population were quite distinct in dress and culture without any need of regulation.

That does not however mean that dhimmitude was a completely invented later development. While many of the rules of dhimmitude emerged in later years, the concept itself did not. Copts and other non-Muslim populations that the Muslims came to rule were expected to pay *jizya*. There has been much modern debate regarding the extent to which *jizya* placed a financial burden on the local population. While some have regarded it as minor and not dissimilar to the tax burden imposed by previous rulers, others have calculated it as amounting to three months' salary per year of a daily worker. The debate over *jizya* as a burden is critical to arguments over reasons for the conversion of non-Muslim populations. Some identify the heavy tax burden as a reason for massive conversions throughout the centuries especially for the poorer Copts who could not afford it and who had three options: conversion to Islam, death, or paying the *jizya*. This would give rise to the modern Coptic narrative that the Copts who clung to their religion and refused to convert were the richer ones, and thus in a sense the better ones. The narrative while not historically accurate—a more

important incentive for conversion was the opportunities it opened
to advancement especially in later centuries—is important to a
sense of self-identity and pride for modern Copts. They were the
ones who paid the price to keep their faith.

But regardless of the financial burden imposed by *jizya,* the
concept and the larger framework of dhimmitude more importantly involved social status. The verse in the Quran referring to
jizya reads as follows: "Fight those who do not believe in Allah,
nor in the latter day, nor do they prohibit what Allah and His
Messenger have prohibited, nor follow the religion of truth, out
of those who have been given the Book, until they pay the *Jizya*
in acknowledgment of superiority and they are in a state of subjection" (Quran 9:29). The last words of the verse would become
the most critical in defining dhimmitude. Non-Muslims were
expected to acknowledge their subjection by acting accordingly.
This entailed an important acknowledgment: an acknowledgment of the superiority of Islam in its land and hence their
inferiority.

The framework of dhimmitude was grounded in a pact supposedly signed between Caliph Omar and Syrian Christians. Its
authenticity has been questioned by scholars, and such a pact is
probably a much later development. The attribution to Omar,
however, would give it legitimacy until this day and result in
attempts at its implementation throughout the centuries. The text
involves a number of conditions that the non-Muslim community
is subjected to and its acknowledgment that breaking those conditions would mean physical harm. These conditions include: promising not to build new churches or monasteries nor renew old ones
that are damaged; promising not to manifest their religion publically, display crosses, or ring loud bells; acting with respect to
Muslims by rising from their seats when a Muslim wishes to sit;
clipping the fronts of their heads; pledging not to imitate Muslims

in their dress; agreeing not to mount on saddles, take Muslims as servants or build houses overtopping Muslim houses.

The enforcement of such regulations grew much stronger in later centuries but signs of such laws already appear in the first period of Umayyad and Abbasid rule. Caliph Yazid II (r. 720–724) ordered the destruction of church icons, while the Abbasid Caliph Al Hadi (r. 785–786) ordered the destruction of churches. During the reign of Caliph Al Mutawakil (r. 847–861) we encounter the first systematic effort of differentiation by means of appearance. The rules would become a model for later generations to follow. Copts were forced to wear hazel-colored clothes with special marks on them, forbidden to ride horses and ordered to use saddles made of wood when mounting other animals, required to hide crosses in marches and funerals, and ordered to put statues and marks of dogs or monkeys on the front of their homes. Besides the subjugation of the non-Muslims, the new regulations especially those regarding dress codes point at marking a distinction between Muslims and non-Muslims. The need for such differentiation reflects increased integration and assimilation between the two communities. Naturally, the major reason for that was the substantial increase of non-Arab Muslims from among the local population through conversion.

THE COPTIC RESPONSE

The new restrictions under Muslim rulers naturally led Copts to develop various responses both challenging and collaborative. The first question Copts faced was that of language. While the first decades of Muslim rule did not require adoption of the Arabic language, it was made the official language in terms of its usage in government service in 705. This forced those Copts planning to make a career in various government services to learn the language of their rulers. At first, the adoption was slow and initially limited to government servants. Later on, Arabic became more widespread, especially after the population balance began to tilt towards Muslims. This led eventually to the decline and near disappearance of the Coptic language.

The second question was that of conversion. When exactly did Egypt become a Muslim majority country? Unfortunately, no clear answer exists. Coptic sources record some instances of conversion during the lives of various popes; these were probably during large waves of conversion which merited their being recorded. We know of such a wave, for example, at the time of Pope Michael I at the end of the Umayyad caliphate when Coptic sources inform us that twenty-four thousand converted. Scholars point to higher levels of conversion under the rule of Omar II, the Umayyad caliph, and under the Abbasid caliphate. Unlike other Umayyad caliphs, Omar removed the *jizya* completely from converts to Islam, thus encouraging conversion as well as increasing the taxation burden on non-Muslims by decreeing that the *jizya* would be collected (from the community as a whole) even on the dead. The Umayyad policy of favoring Arabs over converts was certainly not inducive to conversion. The Abbasid embrace of converts to Islam was thus instrumental in creating a more favorable environment for taking this step. Some scholars point to the end of the ninth and beginning of the tenth century as the time when the population balance began to tip in favor of Muslims, while others point to a later date under Fatimid rule.

The last remaining response to their new condition under Muslim rule was revolution. During the first two centuries of Muslim rule in Egypt, Copts revolted a number of times. Those revolts read more like the last gasps of a dying community than as serious uprisings aimed at removing the Muslims' yoke. One interesting characteristic of these revolts is that most if not all of them occurred in the Nile Delta region and not in the south. Copts in the east of the Delta revolted in 725 and were crushed. Another Delta revolt erupted in the 750s. More important were the revolts by the Bashmurians. The exact location of the Bashmurians is still a matter of debate, though there is broad agreement that they lived in the north of the Delta between the Rosetta and Damietta branches of the Nile in what was marshland. Under the leadership of Mina Ibn Bakira, the Bashmurians were able to benefit from the nature of their land, which made it difficult for armies to conquer. Their fierce insurgency took place during the last years of the Umayyad caliphate. The last hurrah came in 831, when the Caliph Al Ma'mun was forced to personally lead an army against the Bashmurians which resulted in their final defeat.

For its part, the Coptic Church did not play any role in leading its followers in responding to their new status. Coptic sources paint a picture of a church that had accepted the conditions of Muslim rule. Various popes are recorded to have issued requests, often forced to do so by Muslim rulers, asking revolutionaries to put down their arms. Internally we have a picture of a quiet church. No major actions are recorded by the popes living at the time. Nearly all of those popes were selected from among the monks of St. Macarius Monastery in the Western Desert. In 777, at the time of the selection of Pope John IV (r. 777–799), the use of the drawing of lots in the final stage of selecting the new pope is recorded for the first time. This mechanism would be used repetitively throughout the centuries until the present day. An important development affecting the future of the church was the attacks by Berbers on the Western Desert monasteries at the time of Popes Mark II (r. 799–819) and Shenouda I (r. 859–880). The devastation and destruction of the monasteries was a crushing blow to the church. The most important damage to the church's identity, however, occurred in 832, when sailors from Venice stole the body of St. Mark. The return of part of the relics of St. Mark to Egypt in 1968 would be met with wide celebrations.

Survival and Despair

The weakness of the Abbasid caliphate in its later years tempted local governors of Egypt to attempt to separate from its authority and create their own ruling dynasties in Egypt. Though short-lived, those separate dynasties gave Egypt some form of independence both politically and culturally. The Tulunid Dynasty ruled from 868 to 905 and, after a brief thirty-year return to Abbasid rule, the Ikhshidid Dynasty ruled from 935 to 969. It was during Ikhshidid rule that the ruler of Egypt first participated in Coptic festivals, turning them into large celebrations in which the whole population took part. The fall of the Ikhshidids, however, ushered in a new era with the arrival of the Fatimids.

The Fatimid Dynasty claimed descent from the family of the Prophet Mohamed through his daughter Fatima and her husband Ali Ibn Abi Taleb. Ismaili Shi'a Muslims who had founded their caliphate in Tunisia, they soon came to dominate the whole of North Africa. After a number of failed attempts at invading Egypt, they finally succeeded in 969. They built a new city, Cairo, which the Fatimid Caliph Al Muizz Li-Din Allah decided to make his capital. Under Fatimid rule (969–1171) and the Ayyubid Dynasty (1171–1250), a number of major developments took place, both in terms of the position of Copts in Egypt and the internal status of the Coptic Church. The story of Copts in those centuries provides us with the dual dynamic of decline and survival. For some, the story of Copts under Muslim rule revolves around the question of how Copts and their church became weaker until they reached their miserable state at the time of the French invasion. For others, the real question is not how and why Copts descended a downward slope, but how they survived against such overwhelming odds. The two perspectives together provide us with a picture of the dual nature of those years.

The first important development under Fatimid rule was the rise of Coptic state employees who were increasingly allowed to occupy higher positions in the service of the caliphs with some attaining immense power and wealth. Perhaps it was the status of the Fatimids as non-Sunni rulers of a Sunni Muslim population that led them to increasingly depend on non-Muslims as high-ranking bureaucrats. Ultimately, the rise of the Coptic bureaucrats was a source of great frustration and anger among the Muslim population leading to intensified anti-Coptic propaganda and mob attacks. The rise of the Coptic civil servants also meant an increasing dependence of the church on them, shifting the power balance within the church.

The second major development was the relatively open and tolerant policy the Fatimids largely followed. Al Muizz held debates between representatives of the different religions in his palace, where they could argue their respective positions. Some Fatimid caliphs allowed those who had converted to Islam under pressure to return to Christianity, and Al Muizz even intervened forcefully in the face of a Muslim mob to allow Copts to build a church. This tolerant attitude also involved Fatimid caliphs increasingly taking part in Coptic religious celebrations.

Al Muizz plays an important role in church history. According to Copts, one of the greatest miracles occurred due to the religious debates that he hosted. In those debates, a rivalry emerged between Jews and Christians. A Jew,[5] humiliated by an

---

5. Because of the weakness of the Chalcedonians at the time, Copts replaced them with Jews as their primary adversaries in Coptic literature.

earlier exchange, searched the New Testament for material to use against Copts and came across a verse in Matthew's Gospel: "If you have faith as a mustard seed, you will say to this mountain, 'Move from here to there,' and it will move; and nothing will be impossible for you" (Matthew 17:20). Triumphant, he showed it to the caliph who summoned Pope Abraham (r. 975–978) and informed him that unless Copts moved the Mokattam Mountain near Cairo he would order them killed. The whole community is said to have fasted for three days[6] after which the Virgin Mary appeared to the pope and led him to the man who would perform the miracle: Simon the Tanner.[7] With the caliph and his men watching, the mountain was moved, another affirmation according to Copts of the truthfulness of their faith. According to Coptic sources, Al Muizz was so moved by the miracle that he soon abdicated his throne, converted to Christianity, and became a monk.[8]

It was Al Muizz's grandson, Al Hakim Bi-Amr Allah (r. 996–1021), however, who became the greatest persecutor of Copts. A mysterious figure, his life, eccentric character, controversial decisions, and mysterious death continue to fascinate scholars today. In his first few years in office, Al Hakim continued his ancestors' tolerant policy, but in 1004, he suddenly changed his mind. He ordered high-ranking Coptic state employees to convert

---

6. Since that time, those three days have been added to the traditional forty days of fasting before Christmas. Copts till this day observe the Nativity fasting for forty-three days.

7. The story of Simon the Tanner has been revived in recent years with the growth of one of the largest Christian communities in Egypt among the garbage collectors. His church on the Mokattam Mountain is the largest in Egypt and thousands of Christians flock there to pray. It is also today one of the few Orthodox churches that welcomes and holds united Christian prayers across denominations.

8. His baptism is said to have taken place in St. Mercurius Church in Old Cairo. The baptismal font in that church is called the Sultan's Baptistery.

to Islam and killed those who refused. He decreed that Copts were to wear a heavy wooden cross around their necks.[9] Copts were also forced to wear black clothes in differentiation from Muslims and forbidden to wear silk, ride horses, or have Muslim house servants. The caliph then ordered the destruction of churches and confiscated their endowments. In 1009, to the grief of Copts and Christians worldwide, he ordered the destruction of the Holy Sepulcher in Jerusalem. Muslims were not spared his madness. Women were prohibited from appearing in public and dogs were killed.

Al Hakim's persecution led to a massive wave of conversion, although some would later return to Christianity after his death. It is certainly during this period that the population balance finally tilted and Christians no longer constituted a majority of the inhabitants of Egypt. The persecution of Copts flared up again during the coming decades, though nothing would compare to what Copts had experienced under Al Hakim. During the reign of Al Mustansir Billah (r. 1036–1094), churches in Egypt were ordered closed. Saladin's uncle, Shirkuh is recorded by Coptic historians as having initiated a severe persecution in which many Copts were killed, churches burned, and the *jizya* increased.

The relationship between the Egyptian Coptic Church and its daughter churchs in Nubia and Ethiopia continued to be a blessing and a curse for the mother church. While Ethiopian and Nubian rulers continued to plead on behalf of Copts and in some instances were able to better their condition, the fact that the Coptic pope held authority over them led Egypt's rulers to attempt to interfere and control the relationship. Because Ethiopia was the source of the Nile, its Christians became the object of suspicion whenever the Nile flood was lower than expected. Often this led

---

9. The wooden crosses and the pain they caused would give rise to one of the modern derogatory terms that Muslims use to refer to Copts: "blue bone," in reference to the pain marks the heavy crosses made on the Copt's necks.

to the pope's imprisonment. Thus, Pope Zacharias (r. 1004–1032) was forbidden to communicate with Nubia and Ethiopia and Pope Christodolos (r. 1047–1077) was not able to ordain a bishop to Ethiopia. His successor, Pope Cyril II (r. 1078–1092), was forced to ordain a monk chosen by the vizier at the time. Pope John V (r. 1147–1166) was imprisoned for refusing to ordain another bishop to Ethiopia to replace the existing bishop. However, various popes were also used as diplomats by the rulers of Egypt in their relationship with Nubia and Ethiopia. Accordingly, Pope Michael IV (r. 1092–1102) was asked by the caliph to travel to Ethiopia to ask its ruler to allow the Nile to flood at its normal levels. Pope Christodolos was required to write to the king of Nubia urging him to pay the *jizya*.

It was during Fatimid rule that the Christian Crusades to win the Holy Land from the Muslims were launched. They would have an important impact on Christian-Muslim relations as well as the Copts' views of the Catholic Church. Copts were viewed with suspicion by the Muslim rulers and the Muslim population in general. With the crusaders raising the cross and launching a religious war, it was but natural that the loyalty of local Christians became a matter of concern despite the fact that the Copts certainly did not aid the crusaders. Partly this was due to traditional theological differences which made them view the crusaders not as fellow Christians, but as the despised Chalcedonians who had persecuted them earlier. The crusaders' actions further entrenched that view. Copts, who were viewed as heretics by the crusaders were barred from performing pilgrimage to Jerusalem. Furthermore, during their subsequent attempted invasions of Egypt, their brutality did not differentiate between Muslim and Copt. This episode would further entrench the Copt's perception of themselves as a lonely minority, separated not only from their fellow countrymen but from the rest of Christendom as well.

How Have the Mighty Fallen?

The Coptic Church would experience a tremendous decline during this period. The first disastrous development for the quality of its religious teaching was the problem of simony.* Many of the popes of this period practiced simony, sometimes in order to meet the heavy taxation burden put on their shoulders by the rulers, and sometimes out of personal greed. Given that the bishops and priests selected by such popes as Philotheos (r. 979–1003) and Shenouda II (r. 1032–1046) attained their positions only through bribery, it is no surprise that the quality of their knowledge of scripture and theology would be questionable. The church's darkest hour arrived with Pope Cyril III (r. 1235–1243).

At the death of Pope John VI (r. 1189–1216), Daoud Ibn Laqlaq, who would later be known as Cyril III, had actively sought the papal throne, an action frowned upon by Copts who believe that the papacy should be given only to those who do not seek it. Due to his lobbying, active support among some Coptic state employees, and bribes to rulers, he managed to keep the papal throne vacant for nineteen years until all his enemies had died and he was finally enthroned. At last triumphant, Cyril III entered into an ordination spree, ordaining fifty-three bishops using simony. Though a great scholar in his time, his actions and the opposition it aroused would nearly tear the church apart. It is no surprise that after his death Copts did not choose a successor for seven years, while they healed from the wounds he inflicted on the church.

But it was not only simony that affected the quality of preaching in the church. The question of the language of preaching and prayer ignited an important debate inside the church's walls. By

---

* Simony is the act of receiving payment of money in exchange for ordination for various church positions. It is named after Simon Magus who attempted to pay the disciples in order to receive the power of the Holy Spirit.

the time of Pope Gabriel II (r. 1131–1145), the majority of Copts had lost their native language and instead increasingly used Arabic in their daily lives. Traditionalists insisted on maintaining the prayers in their original Coptic form rather than adopting the language of their conquerors. On the other hand, many recognized that with a population now unable to understand prayers and the Bible in Coptic, there was a great risk of them losing any understanding of their faith. Cases began to appear of even priests who were unable to understand Coptic and merely recited the liturgy without comprehending it. Pope Gabriel thus took the controversial decision of ordering readings to be read during liturgy in Arabic. The sad state of Coptic learning was reflected in the fact that his successor as pope, Michael V (r. 1145–1146) was illiterate. As part of this adoption to changing times, Pope Christodolos had made the inevitable step of transferring the seat of the papacy from Alexandria to Cairo. While popes would retain their title of Pope of Alexandria, the need to be closer to the seat of authority in the country has made Cairo their residence ever since.

The rise of a Coptic bureaucratic class in service of Fatimid caliphs led over time to that class adopting many of the social habits of their rulers. The names of those civil servants were thus Arabic names with the glorifications in names common at the time. But more important than names was the lifestyle they adopted. Increasingly we read of Coptic popes and bishops of the time preaching and writing against taking concubines, which had become common among the bureaucrats. The tension between the civil servants and the church authorities manifested themselves on numerous occasions.

Ayyubid rule did not end however before a cultural flourishing occurred within the church. As Copts adopted Arabic as their language, numerous books written in Arabic and dealing with theological and religious subjects emerged during the thirteenth century.

It is during this brief renaissance that Awlad El Assal and Boulos Al Bushy wrote books that remain some of the best Arab Christian literature written.

Their Darkest Hour

If the life of Copts under Fatimid and Ayyubid rule was a mixture of success and despair, the rise of the Mamluks would usher in a period of intense persecution the likes of which they had not yet seen. It was during Mamluk rule that Coptic numbers as a percentage of the overall population shrank nearly to their current levels.

The Mamluks were Turkish, Georgian, and Circassian slaves bought by rulers at a young age and trained to become a warrior class. While various rulers had obtained such slaves in the past, it was under the Ayyubid Dynasty that the phenomenon would be greatly expanded. With the death of the last Ayyubid ruler, the Mamluks took over power themselves establishing a sultanate that continued for three centuries until finally falling to Ottoman invaders in 1517. Though defeated by the Ottomans, they would soon regain their strength and continue to play a major role in Egyptian politics until Mohamed Ali finally massacred them in 1811.

Life in Egypt under the Mamluks was one of endless disasters that befell the population at large and especially Copts. Throughout the three centuries of their rule, and due to the lack of any rules of succession except might, Mamluks were in endless skirmishes and wars with each other. Egypt was ruled by fifty-four sultans during those 267 years many of whom spent less than a year in power. Continuous internal wars and competition meant that each Mamluk aimed to use his fiefdom to gather the largest amount of money in order to finance his quest for the throne.

If their rulers were not already a reason for their plight, nature provided Egyptians with more reasons for sorrow. Continuous low floods from the Nile meant smaller crops and as a result numerous famines. Severe inflations brought havoc upon the country. By the end of Mamluk rule, a further catastrophe befell Egypt in the form of Portugal's discovery of the route to India via the Cape of Good Hope. This great discovery for Europe meant a grave loss for Egypt as a trade route in the form of tolls and taxes. Attempts by the Mamluks to fight the Portuguese in the Red Sea proved futile. Soon, their own rule fell to the invading Ottoman army.

Egypt under Ottoman rule witnessed further decline. After conquering Egypt, Sultan Selim I, took with him to Istanbul the country's finest skilled laborers resulting in a collapse in many trades. The Ottomans, ruling a vast empire, had little interest in the welfare of their Egyptian province, leaving the reorganized Mamluks to compete for power with a succession of frequently changed Ottoman governors. The end of Egypt as a trade route coupled with continued famines led to the country's decline in every aspect.

Under Mamluk rule, the persecution of Copts intensified. Previous patterns of persecution continued. Baibars (r. 1260–1267) is reported to have gathered all Copts in Cairo and attempted to burn them together with the city's Jews, only to be stopped at the last minute after pleas by some Mamluk princes. He further re-imposed the dress codes on Copts. The re-imposition of the codes on this and numerous subsequent instances highlights the fact that they were not closely followed. A wave of persecution and reemphasis of dress differentiation would be followed by more lenient rulers and the relaxation of the dress codes. Other forms of persecution continued, with popes often paying the price in the form of arrests and beatings.

But if previous persecution patterns continued, new ones emerged during Mamluk times. The Cairo mob became an active participant and instigator of persecution often demanding the imposition of more restrictions. What explains this new phenomenon? Some scholars point to an intensification of Sunni religious culture during this period; others highlight the fact that, as strangers to the country, the Mamluks needed to portray themselves as the defenders of the faith, both from foreign threats and from the non-Muslim minority's perceived attempts to go beyond its accepted social position.

Most importantly, at the center of the mob's anger stood the Coptic civil servants who had become indispensable for the Mamluks. The nature and patterns of this resentment reminds us of modern anti-Semitism. The Coptic civil servant class was viewed as closed, with the secrets of the job passed within. Muslims, especially newly converted ones naturally felt hatred towards the position the Coptic civil servants enjoyed. The mob would often spur into action after an incident where a Coptic civil servant was perceived to have forgotten his place by riding a horse, wearing silk clothing, or simply walking proudly. The mob would start by attacking that Copt and then enter a rampage of burning and looting Coptic homes and churches. Such an incident took place in 1300 and ignited a strong wave of persecution that lasted for two years.

The second aspect of the mob action that bears resemblance to modern anti-Semitism is the constant suspicion that trailed new converts from among the civil servants class. Due to persecution many Coptic civil servants found it expedient to convert. Their conversion was viewed with suspicion from the mob who would often demand that they still be removed from their positions until their adherence to Islam was manifested and tested. This notion of perceiving them as Copts even after their conversion led some of the converted civil servants to be overzealous and persecute their previous co-religionists in an attempt to appear as more authentic Muslims.

Furthermore, in another interesting aspect of the mob violence against Copts, the usage of propaganda appears for the first time, with pamphlets distributed and speeches given attacking Copts. Rumors and perceived conspiracies were also instrumental in igniting mob action. In 1321, after several fires in Cairo, a number of Copts were arrested and blamed for them, which ignited another wave of mob action that resulted in hundreds of deaths and tens of churches destroyed. The various waves of persecution took their toll on the community and its churches. A recent study[10] records a devastating decline in the number of churches from 2048 in 1200 to a mere 112 in 1600.

While Mamluk rulers were no friends of the Copts, they certainly preferred their organized traditional methods of persecution which would allow them to extort money from the Copts to the uncontrolled mob actions. They were however often at a loss as to how to control the mob. As a means of maintaining order, they had to give in until the storm would pass. Thus mob action would be accompanied by the re-imposition of stricter dress and behavioral codes. The dress code was thus imposed during the papacy of John VII (r. 1271–1293), blue turbans were imposed after the 1300 riots as well as an increase in the *jizya* and banning Copts from riding horses. The problem of riding horses returns as a key issue during the papacy of Mark IV (r. 1348–1363), black clothes and turbans are imposed during the papacy of John XIV (r. 1571–1586), blue is imposed at the time of Mark VI (r. 1646–1656) with

---

10. Guirguis, Magdi and Nelly van Doorn-Harder, *The Emergence of the Modern Coptic Papacy.*

restriction on riding horses returning. Black is again imposed during John XVI's papacy (r. 1676–1718) as well as wearing bells around the neck and forbidding Copts to wear woolen clothing. A ban on using names that are used by Muslims is imposed at the time of Pope John XVIII (r. 1769–1796). Before that a new restriction banning Coptic doctors from examining Muslim patients joins the long list of prohibited actions.

Other means to placate the mob were also used. Sometimes they took the form of giving the mob a free rein for a few days to terrorize Copts and loot their property. In 1300, it was proclaimed that whoever killed a Copt could claim that Copt's wealth, and churches were ordered closed. New taxes were imposed on Copts during Gabriel IV's papacy (r. 1370–1378). Yet the central Mamluk action to appease the street anger had to deal with the root of that anger, the Coptic civil servants. With Coptic civil servants viewed by the mob as the source of all misfortunes that befell the country, taking actions against them was an appropriate scapegoat for public anger. Every wave of anti-Coptic riots would mean a decision by the Mamluks to fire Coptic civil servants. This happened repeatedly during the papacies of John VIII (r. 1300–1320), Mark IV, and John XI (r. 1427–1452). The fact that the decree firing the civil servants had to be repeated naturally points out that it was hardly followed. The Mamluks were dependent on these Coptic civil servants and once the mob violence receded, life was again back to normal. However, the pressure was enormous on these civil servants to convert and many of them did. Conversion in Mamluk Egypt was a complicated phenomenon driven by many motives from conviction to coercion. For some it involved a calculated decision to seek a better future, while for others simply the last stage of a process of association and intermingling with Muslims.

THE CHALLENGE BEGINS

The continuous drain on the richest segment of the Coptic community, the civil servants, meant that the church and the community at large were severely impacted. The loss of rich community members meant fewer donations, less giving to the poor, and less money available for popes to pay off greedy Mamluks and governors. It also meant a continuous loss of the better-educated elements in the community. The impact of that depletion meant further decline in the quality of learning and preaching inside the church. Social habits that had plagued the church since Fatimid times continued and were further entrenched. Copts in the Delta claimed during the papacy of Mark V (r. 1603–1619) that Christians could practice polygamy. The pope's attempt to stop them ended with him in prison. His successor John XV (r. 1619–1629) was killed by a rich Copt for refusing to endorse the by then widespread phenomenon of taking concubines.

This is not to say that the church was bereft of any bright spot. During its darkest days, there were some bright lights such as Pope Matthew I (r. 1378–1408) who was known for his piety, almsgiving, and humility. There were also several martyrs who refused to give up their faith and provided an example that the community would remember and celebrate. Two non-monks, yet living a life of poverty and prayer, would become among the most famous Coptic saints: Anba Barsoum El Erian and Anba Rowais.

Nevertheless the greatest challenge to the Coptic Church came in the form of the return of an old enemy, the Chalcedonians. The Melkites had certainly never disappeared from Egypt. After an interval at the time of the Arab invasion, Melkite patriarchs were consecrated at Alexandria and led their small community of followers. Various clashes with the Coptic Church took place throughout the centuries, but given the weakness of the Byzantine Empire and the small number of their followers in Egypt, they never posed a serious threat to the Coptic Church. The Roman Catholic Church was quite another story.

Catholic attempts to convert Copts to Catholicism first targeted the Ethiopian church. The search for Prester John, the imaginary medieval great Christian king, had led some to associate the legend with the Christian kingdom in Ethiopia. Simultaneously kings of Ethiopia were seeking help from Christian kingdoms in Europe in their wars with their Muslim neighbors. Portuguese explorers, Catholic missionaries, and traders all made their way to the isolated kingdom and brought Catholicism with them. Coptic sources reported the first sign of trouble during the papacy of John VIII, with a brief mention of the Ethiopian people rejecting Catholic missionaries. It was however under Pope John XIII (r. 1484–1524) that the conversion attempts would begin in earnest. Jesuit missionaries arrived in 1555, and by 1603, the Ethiopian Emperor Za Dengal (r. 1603–1604) converted to Catholicism. The Coptic bishop encouraged the rebellion which soon toppled him. Catholic attempts again succeeded in 1622 in converting Emperor Sesenyos (r. 1606–1632) leading to another outbreak of religious fighting within Ethiopia as the population refused to follow its emperor and, led by its local clergy, rebelled. Catholic missionaries were finally kicked out after Sesenyos's death, though the Roman pontiff and Catholic kings of Europe continued their attempts to convert Ethiopians.

The episode in Ethiopia was only the beginning of increased Catholic interest in the Coptic Church. Gabriel VII (r. 1525–1570) was the first to receive emissaries sent by the Roman pontiff with a suggestion of a unity between the two churches. Unity, naturally, was not understood as one between equals, but as the Coptic Church submitting itself to the authority of the pope in Rome. The two main obstacles for such a unity to take place were the old feud over the nature of Christ as well as the Catholic belief in the primacy of Peter and hence the primacy of the pope in Rome, which the Coptic Church continued to reject. Emissaries returned again during the papacy of his successor John XIV, who convened a synod of the Coptic Church to decide on the matter. With the synod split, and the pope rumored to be in favor, his death was attributed by Catholics to those opposed to the unity. The two subsequent popes, Gabriel VIII (r. 1587–1603) and Mark V, were also at the receiving end of Roman attempts to bring the Coptic Church under the Holy See, with both rejecting the venture. The attempts receded for a while, but were soon continued at the time of Pope John XVI.

If the attempts at official unity had failed, the effort soon started to convert the Coptic population. In 1630, the first Capuchin missionaries arrived in Egypt and were soon followed in quick pace by the Franciscans in 1632, and the Jesuits in 1675. The missionaries were able not only to enjoy the protection of the Western powers' representatives but also to make use of the foreign capitulations that the Ottoman Empire began granting to European powers. Under that protection they were able to bring their message to the south of Egypt and began converting Copts. Two important defections in 1741 and 1758 by two Coptic bishops led to further growth in the numbers of Coptic converts. Coptic fears of Catholic conversion efforts led them to appeal to the Mamluks to stop them in 1738. This appeal to the rulers in order to prevent missionaries from operating would be attempted repeatedly in the future.

Soon, some of the young Catholic converts were sent for education in Rome leading to growing translation work there from Coptic manuscripts. The onslaught by Western travellers on Coptic monasteries led to thousands of Coptic manuscripts making their way to Europe. Later on during the nineteenth and twentieth centuries, Copts would look back with bitterness at the depletion of their monasteries from their historical treasures at the hands of European adventurers.

As the eighteenth century was coming to a close, Egypt was in a state of hibernation. The country's population had shrunk tremendously due to successive famines and pandemics. Egypt had become a neglected province of the Ottoman Empire left to continuous fighting between Ottoman governors and Mamluk beys. The fall of the country's fortunes was mirrored in the decline of education, knowledge, health, and culture. Like the country at large, the Coptic Church had caught all the diseases of the Middle Ages: the level of religious learning was weak, priests were illiterate and performed the liturgy by memorizing it. The church was being challenged at home and abroad in Ethiopia by Catholic missionaries and, at that moment, was ill-equipped to face them.

CHAPTER THREE

Corsican General,
Albanian Commander

"Forty Centuries of History Contemplate You"[1]

B Y THE BEGINNING OF THE EIGHTEENTH CENTURY Ottoman control of Egypt was eroding. Sultan Selim I had placed
those Mamluks who swore loyalty to him in control of the
provinces, while leaving behind an Ottoman garrison to balance
their power. Ottoman governors would be sent from Istanbul in
quick succession, each never staying longer than two or three years.
With the Mamluks still allowed to buy new slaves, they were able
to continuously strengthen their ranks and soon absorb the Ottoman garrison. Governors were never able to consolidate enough
power during their short terms in Egypt to curb Mamluk power.
By the eighteenth century, they were ruling Egypt in name only
with real control in the hands of Mamluk beys, whose continuous internal divisions ensured that none of them would be powerful enough to consider challenging Ottoman sovereignty over
the country.

The equilibrium was shattered with the rise of Ali Bey Al Kabir
(1728–1773). Ali Bey was taken from his family in Georgia and

---

1. Later histories claimed that Napoleon had said those words to his
soldiers before the Battle of the Pyramids. The quote is likely a later
fabrication.

sold as a slave at the age of thirteen.[2] He rose quickly in Mamluk ranks and by 1768 had become the leader of the Mamluks. Unlike other Mamluks, who were consistently preoccupied with petty fights between them, Ali Bey harbored larger dreams. Grasping the significance of world politics he aimed to use it to his advantage. Sensing an opportunity with war breaking out between the Ottoman Empire and Russia, he removed the Ottoman governor, signed treaties with Venice and Russia, and declared the independence of Egypt. His dream seemed to be materializing with the Ottomans helpless before his advancing army in Syria that was further aided by a local coalition he had built. However, his dream was short-lived, as his leading Mamluk commander betrayed him, leading to his eventual death and putting an end to this brief moment of independence. During his short lived project, Ali Bey had encouraged Syrian Catholics to immigrate to Egypt and gave them control of the customs office, replacing the Jews. A Copt, Moalem Rizk, rose to prominence as the manager of Ali Bey's finances. Ali Bey's project however was not driven by a modernizing dream. While he certainly aimed at Egypt's independence and possibly the reestablishment of Mamluk control of Syria and the Hejaz, his project is analogous to historical attempts by local governors of Muslim provinces to secede from the center. Modernization was not sought, nor was it yet envisioned.

The Egypt where Napoleon landed in 1798 was in a state of stagnation. Centuries had passed Egypt by hardly leaving their mark. The country's economy had declined tremendously and so

---

2. How much of their previous lives the young Mamluks remembered was an open question. Kidnapped from their Christian families and sold in Egypt at a young age, some of them, certainly the older ones, probably remembered their lives before becoming Mamluks. In the case of Ali Bey, kidnapped at such an old age, we can certainly assume that he remembered a lot. After his demise, he would be accused of secretly being a Christian.

had the population. Agriculture was the main economic activity with few small industries. Education was provided through the *kuttab* system as it had for centuries before, with Al Azhar providing the only available higher education. The quality of Al Azhar education had deteriorated tremendously, sciences were hardly taught, and memorization was the method of teaching. Coptic primary education was a bit better than that of the rest of the population, with Coptic *kuttabs* teaching geometry and arithmetic to its students to prepare them for their future jobs. Copts were employed by the Mamluks as secretaries, accountants, land surveyors, and tax collectors. Cultural life in Egypt was limited to Quran recital during religious occasions and few gatherings hosted by Mamluk beys. While some modern weapons had made their way to Egypt, the Mamluks continued to engage in warfare with a medieval mindset. No Egyptian took part in the battles that often occurred between Mamluks as the affairs of the state were not theirs.

The control of the country had fallen into the hands of two Mamluks: Ibrahim Bey and Murad Bey. The Ottomans, attempting to put an end to Mamluk independence, had sent a military force that forced both beys to flee to the south of the country. While quite brutal, especially to Copts, who were forced to pay heavy fines and abide by the dress codes, the force failed to bring an end to the Mamluk control and Ibrahim and Murad were soon back in Cairo.

Nelson had beat Napoleon to the shores of Alexandria and attempted to warn the residents of the city and authorities of the incoming invasion and offer them assistance. The British warning fell on deaf ears. They were rebuked. The rulers of Egypt needed no assistance they were told; if the French came they would be defeated. The hubris continued even after news reached Cairo of Napoleon landing in Alexandria with his large army on July 1, 1798.

While Copts were viewed as possible traitors with their homes attacked and searched, no real effort was undertaken to organize a serious defense in face of the invading army. A Mamluk is quoted as saying: "Let all the Franks come and we shall crush them beneath our horses' hooves." To the utter shock of the Mamluks and the Egyptians hearing the news, when the two armies met, first in the Battle of Shubra Khit and then in the Battle of the Pyramids on July 21, it was the Mamluks who were crushed and forced to flee.

The shock was profound. The armies of the East and the West had met in battle and the results were astounding. The French lost twenty-nine men compared to an estimated two thousand Mamluks. The Franks, whom the Mamluks had last met during the Crusades, were not the same men as those led by Louis IX. Instead of the crusader knight, the Mamluks now faced the modern French army. The enormous changes that had taken place in Europe during the preceding centuries were completely alien to the Mamluks and the Egyptian population at large. When the two armies met, the Egyptians were expecting a battle along the lines they remembered from the Crusades. Ottoman victories in Europe, reaching the gates of Vienna twice, had reinforced the sense of comfort in the supremacy of Islam and its armies.

Napoleon attempted to reach out to the local population. His first proclamation declared him as a friend of the Ottoman Sultan, who had come to rid Egypt from the Mamluks. He proclaimed his high regard of Islam, highlighted how he was an enemy of Christendom by stressing his invasion of Rome and crushing of the Knights of Malta. He stressed to his troops the need to respect Islam and its customs. His immediate task was to organize the government of the country to ensure its continued functioning. He established a *diwan* (council), which included local notables and, in a novelty, leading Christian civil servants. Naturally the goal was not the establishment of a democracy guided by principles of equality and liberty, but to ensure local cooperation. Napoleon's goal was the better management of the country's affairs to serve his plans and not the liberation of Egypt from the Ottoman yoke. The change however was dramatic. For the preceding centuries, a change of governor or ruler was merely a change in name. The country was ruled in the same manner. For the first time a new system of organization and government was introduced.

Napoleon's relationship with the Copts was not friendly. Given their small numbers, the Muslim majority was the constituency that he cared about. His outreach to Muslims certainly did not please Copts, who were in all cases not favorably disposed towards Europeans due to memories of persecutions at the hands of the Chalcedonians, the crusaders episode, and their historical isolation. If any of them felt a common cause with their fellow European Christians, Napoleon put an end to their hopes. He realized that they would not be on his enemies' side and thus put little effort into courting their support. He never trusted the Coptic civil servants and hoped to remove them from collecting taxes, a task his successors achieved two years later. He was clearly aware that any favorable policy towards Copts would anger Muslims, yet he found himself in a delicate position given the absurdity of the rules by which Copts were governed. While attempting to keep a balance between toleration towards Copts and appeasing Muslims, Napoleon's policy was shattered by reality. Those Copts who were emboldened by the French rule started riding horses and carrying weapons in public, both considered a serious breach of their status as *dhimmis*. El Gabarty (1753–1825), the Egyptian historian who lived during those years, wrote quite angrily about Copts and Syrian Christians acting as if they were equals and insulting Islam by their conduct. The awkwardness of his policy was evident when he ordered Christians to refrain from wearing white turbans and publically breaking the fast during Ramadan, while at the same time informing their leaders that he was favorably disposed towards them.

Though Napoleon attempted to build bridges with local sheikhs and win their trust, they nevertheless incited the mob to attack French soldiers, as well as Copts at the first sign of Ottoman armies coming close to Cairo. Historians recorded the brutal attacks that befell Copts during the Ottoman advance on Cairo. While Napoleon attempted to win Egyptians to his side by playing on a sense of Egyptian nationalism, his failure can be traced to the lack of existence of such a feeling. Putting aside the fact that he was an occupier, the population continued to view him through the prism of their worldview, as a non-Muslim. No matter how secular he was, or how favorable to Islam he portrayed himself, he was still a non-Muslim and any benefit his rule brought was far outweighed by that fact. El Gabarty was angered by Copts forgetting their rightful place as he was with the immorality that the French spread with them. Women started appearing in public, mixing with the French soldiers and imitating the French both in their clothes and conduct. This grave insult to tradition and morality annoyed El Gabarty the most.

Napoleon had brought with him 167 French scientists who would later write the famous "*Description de l'Egypte.*" Their work in Egypt is credited by later generations of Egyptians with introducing Egyptians to modern technology and opening their eyes to the gap that existed between them and Europe. Francophiles, and most of the future Egyptian intellectual class were favorably disposed to France, thus saw the invasion as a beacon of light that lifted Egypt from the dark ages. Such a reading suffers from the common disease of reading the past with modern eyes and imagining that people at the time viewed things the way we view them today.

Very few Egyptians actually had direct contact with the French scientists or were impressed by them. Sheikh Hassan El Attar,

who would later lead Al Azhar during Mohamed Ali's rule, was
certainly influenced by them but few others were. El Gabarty
sometimes describes scientific wonders as childish games intended
to impress Egyptians. In a famous episode, Napoleon, keen on
impressing his new friends, invited a number of Al Azhar sheikhs
to attend a chemical experiment, expecting to have a good laugh at
their expense. Instead, they watched the experiment, their faces
lacking any expression. When the experiment ended, one of them
asked Napoleon whether his scientist could make him travel from
Egypt to Morocco in one second, to which Naploeon replied in
the negative. The sheikh then informed him that then his man was
obviously not a good magician.

That is not to say that the French had zero impact on life in
Egypt; they did. Faced with the spread of diseases, the French
introduced Egyptians to modern methods of disease prevention
by quarantining the sick, banning burials inside the cities, and
ordering the streets cleaned. They also attempted to record births,
marriages, and deaths. French scientists roamed the country looking for projects to improve agricultural production such as building dams and envisioning the idea of digging a canal between the
Mediterranean and Red Sea. The French also discovered their fascination with ancient Egypt which began the study of Egyptology.
French rules, however, were viewed as an unwelcome interference
in people's private lives. While Mamluk rule was brutal and life
was unstable, people were largely left to their own devices. The
French attempt to bring organization to the country meant an
intrusion into the lives of ordinary Egyptians.

The most important development was the collapse of the sense
of comfort that people had in the superiority of Islam's armies.
Though the French would be forced to leave in three years, the
Mamluks were never able to regain their power and control over
the country. Their quick defeat and the fact that Napoleon had

been able to conquer the north of the country and Cairo in less than a month shattered the myth of their superiority. Nor did the Ottomans perform any better. Though they were vastly superior in numbers, Ottoman armies sent to defeat the French were crushed by Napoleon and Kleber, who succeeded him in commanding French troops after Napoleon fled to France. While the Ottoman armies were able to terrorize Copts and kill many of them, they were ultimately proven to be less advanced than the French. It was only due to British control of the Mediterranean and the lack of supply routes from France that the French were forced to surrender and leave. Those two lessons, the weakness of Muslim armies, and the importance of world politics, would not be forgotten and would inform the worldview of Mohamed Ali.

THE FIRST EGYPTIAN?

One man however stands out and deserves special attention: General Yacoub. Moalem Yacoub Hanna was born in 1745 and like other Copts was educated as a civil servant. He entered into the service of a Mamluk, Suliman Bey, eventually overseeing his finances. But even before the French invasion, Yacoub was clearly different from the rest of the Coptic civil servants. He married a Syrian woman which was quite uncommon at the time. More importantly, he seems to have sought to play a role larger than that given to the Coptic accountant and secretary. He learned how to ride horses and use swords and is mentioned as having taken part in his master's battles. It was, however, with the French invasion that his world was completely turned upside down. Initially continuing in his role as a financier, he was attached to General Desaix who led a force to conquer the south of Egypt and defeat the Mamluks that had gathered there. Yacoub soon befriended Desaix, and distinguished himself in the battle of Ain El Qousia. Desaix, recognizing his talents, made him his special advisor and involved him in the military campaign. Desaix appears to have been more intellectually open than the rest of the French officers. Accounts describe him holding open discussions among his staff, including Yacoub, where the ideas of the French Revolution were debated. As would later be evident, Yacoub was greatly influenced by those discussions.

Yacoub, probably encouraged by Desaix, formed a Coptic Legion to fight at the side of the French. The very notion of arming and training Copts was shocking. Egyptians, in general, had not taken part in military affairs since at least Ayyubid times and Copts since much earlier at the time of the Muslim invasion. Yacoub recruited two thousand Copts from Upper Egypt, probably through coercion. They were given uniforms and military training by French officers. Yacoub was himself made a general and the head of his legion. This Coptic Legion, as it came to be called, came in handy when the Ottomans tried to retake Egypt and the Cairo population revolted against the French. While other areas where Copts lived were looted and Copts murdered, Yacoub barricaded himself in the Cairo neighborhood of Azbakiya and defended Copts there successfully.

With the French forced to withdraw from Egypt, the fate of those who had helped them became a matter of great concern. Articles 12 and 13 of the treaty they signed included protection for those who had helped them and chose to remain as well as allowing anyone who wished to leave with them for France to do so. Those who stayed soon enough discovered the Ottomans' commitment to the treaty and were murdered. General Yacoub initially planned on staying and mounting a defense on his own of Egypt but soon changed his mind and decided to leave. He attempted to take his Coptic troops with him, but most of them prevailed upon the French commanders to allow them to stay. Yacoub, accompanied by his immediate family and some of his troops and supporters left on British ships heading to France. He left Egypt on August 10, 1801, and died six days later at sea. It was however in those six days aboard the ship that he would make his greatest claim to fame.

On the ship, using as interpreter an adventurous French officer of Maltese origin by the name of Theodore Lascaris, General Yacoub befriended the British captain. The British archives hold two documents, one a report by the ship captain to his superiors in London about the conversations he had with General Yacoub and his impressions of the man and his views, the second an official letter from Lascaris. Once they reached France, two more letters were addressed to Napoleon and the French foreign minister in the name of the Egyptians. Together those four documents represent the earliest project for the independence of Egypt.

The first important aspect of those letters is that Yacoub is presented as head of an Egyptian delegation that aims to contact European powers to seek the independence of Egypt. We have no proof that Yacoub was tasked by the Muslim notables who despised him or the Coptic civil servants who were weary of him to negotiate anything. The claim of heading a delegation is certainly an attempt to impress. Nevertheless the letters are remarkable, both in the novelty of the ideas they contain and in how similar these are to those underlying future Egyptian attempts to gain independence.

The Egypt portrayed in these documents is one of past glory, its current state of affairs a horrible fate for a people who built a great civilization. The letters play on the theme of the debt humanity has to that ancient civilization. Emphasis on that theme is employed to argue that there is hope for Egypt's future, which has the potential to be a great nation once again. The letters build a humanitarian and moral argument in support of Egypt's independence but they also present the practicalities of the matter. In the letter addressed to Britain, British benefits of Egypt's independence are highlighted with the French letter highlighting benefits to France. The letters are based on the notion of negotiations with the great powers to gain independence. Such a method would be the hallmark of Egyptian efforts for the coming 150 years. They also argue that Egypt is too important to fall under one European power and thus that it is in everyone's benefit to help its independence. Some practical matters such as the form of government the newly independent Egypt would take and how it would defend itself are mentioned though in abstract and brief terms.

Was Yacoub a visionary, a man who was not understood by his contemporaries? Was he the first Egyptian nationalist or a traitor who collaborated with the invaders? His character and actions would remain a topic of heated debate until the present. Contemporary Coptic writers present him as a hero, a Coptic/Egyptian nationalist, a man who saw the light before any of his countrymen. On the other hand, the name General Yacoub would be used by Islamist writers to prove Copts' historical treason and to slander any Copt standing in their way by portraying him as a traitor to Egypt who was working with and for its enemies.[3] General Yacoub represents the clearest example of the impact the French invasion had on people's mindset. Such themes as the glory of ancient Egypt were certainly acquired from his interactions with the French. Yacoub was undoubtedly a man well ahead of his times. Those of his Coptic Legion who accompanied him to France continued to fight in its army, several of them achieving high ranks.

----

3. The most recent example is Naguib Sawiris, the Coptic businessman who played a leading role in forming the non-Islamist Egyptian Bloc. The Muslim Brotherhood website portrays Sawiris as the modern General Yacoub.

The Coptic Legion was finally disbanded on September 29, 1814. The renowned educator Rifa'a El Tahtawi, who was in Paris in 1826, wrote in his famous book, *talkhis al-ibriz fi talkhis Bariz*, about his encounter with some of them.

While General Yacoub is today celebrated by Coptic writers as a hero and his actions are highly praised, Copts in his time were not as enthusiastic. Coptic writers at the end of the nineteenth century found a lot to praise in his contemporary Coptic civil servants but not in him. Moalem Ibrahim El Gohary was celebrated for being close to the church, for having helped secure Ottoman decrees for the building of churches, and for giving lots of money and 283 endowments to the church. Other Coptic civil servants were praised along the same lines. Yacoub, on the other hand, is not recorded to have helped the church in any way. No endowment is recorded to have been given by him. His relationship with the church seems to have been problematic even before the French invasion, as it appears that his marriage was not recognized as official.[4] His efforts to form the Coptic Legion meant taking men away from their families. Early Coptic accounts record the story of his clash with the Coptic pope during the French invasion which reached its dramatic climax with General Yacoub entering a church during the liturgy on his horse with his weapons and demanding to be given communion. Perhaps his contemporaries and the pope were much wiser. After all, they knew quite well that the French would eventually leave and that they would once again return under Muslim rule and answer for their actions during French rule.

---

4. While no reason is given for that other than that his wife was Syrian, one may assume that she was Catholic and this is why the church did not recognize the marriage.

"I HAVE NOTHING TO LEARN FROM MACHIAVELLI"

The vacuum created by the French withdrawal generated an opening for Mohamed Ali. An Albanian, he had come to Egypt as part of the Ottoman forces sent to expel the French. Fortune and cunning pushed him to the center of the struggle to rule Egypt and elevated him to be a prime contender. Through a combination of mistakes by his competitors and his own outreach to the *ulama* (Muslim religious scholars) and other notables he was able to ascend to the governorship of Egypt in 1805. Today, Mohamed Ali is hailed by Egyptians as the founder of modern Egypt. This reputation is unsubstantiated. Without a doubt, Egypt went through enormous changes under his rule that had a lasting impact on its future historical development. However, a close examination of the nature of those changes and the driving rationale behind them leaves little doubt that "modern Egypt" is a much later development.

Modernity and its discontents were certainly not the driving force behind Mohamed Ali's reforms. He himself cannot be described as a modern man. Both his conceptions of the world and his method of ruling followed traditional patterns. The changes that he introduced were largely a result of necessity and to serve his one goal, to strengthen his military. The short-lived French invasion seems to have taught Mohamed Ali an important lesson: that Egypt had become central to world politics. As a result, Egypt could not afford to return to its isolation and tranquility. If Egypt ignored the world, the world would not ignore it in return. Sooner or later, the Europeans would be coming back. This understanding was reinforced by the failed British campaign of 1807. As a result, Egypt had to be defended. As the Europeans had mastered the arts of war, it was from their book that Egypt was to copy.

While Egypt's defenses were undoubtedly on Mohamed Ali's mind, so was his own personal advancement. A strong military was not only necessary for the defense of Egypt against Western invasions but also for strengthening Mohamed Ali's position in Egypt as he aimed to solidify his internal rule and gain as much independence as he could from the Ottoman Sultan. Building a strong military, however, was easier said than done.

The first obvious obstacle was the lack of men available for conscription. His own Mamluks were not numerous enough to form a large army and his Albanian soldiers proved untrustworthy. Attempts to recruit Sudanese and train them as soldiers proved unsuccessful. Whatever men he had at his disposal proved inadequate especially because he soon found himself involved in various military campaigns at the behest of his Ottoman master, first in the Arabian desert and then in Greece. In the end, the only available, largely unlimited pool of soldiers was the Egyptian people.

Mohamed Ali's misgivings about recruiting Egyptians stemmed from his fear that it would affect the economic production level, which was essential to sustaining a large army. Whatever his doubts, he was finally forced to conscript Egyptian peasants, a decision that would have profound implications. At the height of his power in 1840, Mohamed Ali's army was 250,000 strong. While the officers were non-Egyptians, the sheer number of troops involved meant that more than 10 percent of the Muslim male population of Egypt was in arms. Conscripted into the military, those men's lives were shattered. They were taken from their villages against their will, uprooted from their familiar surroundings where their ancestors had lived for centuries, thrown into a training process and then into battlefields far from their homes in Arabia, Sudan, Greece, Syria, and modern Turkey. While this did not mean a complete opening to social advancement, the social mobility it entailed was unprecedented. An entire generation had been uprooted from their traditional lives. They had not been made into modern men, but the impact was still enormous.

Tens of thousands of soldiers, however, were not enough to build an army capable of implementing Mohamed Ali's grandiose plans and defending Egypt. Those soldiers needed officers and training in modern methods of warfare. Neither was available in the Egypt that Mohamed Ali ruled. It was inevitable that, lacking qualified men, Mohamed Ali would seek talented officers abroad to train and lead his soldiers. While the end of the Napoleonic wars surely meant the availability of many officers, the quality of those attracted to a job in Egypt was not always of the best caliber. Adventurous souls, seekers of glory and fortunes, and fraudulent characters were all readily available.

A modern army required an endless supply of ammunition, weapons, and clothing. To provide for his army's needs, Mohamed Ali began the process of industrialization in Egypt. In an obvious divergence from the European road to modernity, industrialization in Egypt was not started by an independent bourgeoisie but was entirely a state enterprise. Similarly it was not governed by rules of supply and demand. Mohamed Ali was the sole producer and the buyer. His buying habits were of a specific nature: military. This meant that resources were allocated based not on market mechanisms, but on military needs. It also explains the subsequent collapse of the industries Mohamed Ali built after 1840 when he was forced to dramatically reduce the size of the Egyptian army to only 18,000 men. With no army to serve, the industries were closed one after the other.

The training of soldiers was not restricted to military skills. A large modern army required good doctors to treat the soldiers, excellent veterinarians for the animals, well-trained metal workers, and a variety of other skills. But before a young man could be trained as a doctor or an engineer, he first had to be able to read and write. The state of education in Egypt was obviously a major obstacle in implementing Mohamed Ali's purposes. If Mohamed Ali harbored any dream of building a modern army, education was a must.

Mohamed Ali's educational policy involved various steps. First, at the height of the dream, forty-seven primary schools were opened throughout the country. Together they had about five thousand students. Education was quite basic and, given the continuous need for new students for the more advanced schools, very few were actually able to receive a full primary education. The more advanced schools were developed as the military need for them emerged. Schools of artillery, infantry, cavalry, navy, medicine, pharmaceutics, irrigation, engineering, mineralogy, signaling, veterinary, and officers were opened. In all of these schools, education was provided by foreign nationals who nearly unanimously could not speak the language of their pupils, be it Turkish or Arabic. As a result, instruction was provided through translators. One key weakness in the educational system was precisely the lack of the word system. Foreigners were recruited from across Europe with no particular system in mind to copy. Foreign teachers were often at odds with each other, and beset by interference from their country's representatives in Egypt, each trying to better his nationals' fortunes.

It was, however, the decision to send students abroad that would receive the most acclaim from later generations. The first student was sent quite early in 1809 with twenty-seven others following him by 1818. In 1826, the decision was taken to send a large group of students at the same time. This first educational mission included forty-four students. It was soon followed by other missions in 1828, 1829, 1832. Those four missions comprised 152 students. Students included a combination of Turks, Armenians, and Egyptian Muslims. No Copt was sent. The educational missions naturally followed Mohamed Ali's overall goal, with the students studying military science, printing, ship building, and manufacturing. None of these students was allowed to study arts, for example, or social sciences. Upon their return, the students were given employment in the military, civil service, and some in education. These early pioneers were not welcomed back home as national heroes. On the contrary, they were despised by most. To the foreigners, these students were no more than competitors who one day would take their places, while the Turkish civil servants viewed them as Westernized. To add insult to injury, many of them were not appointed in the most suitable place for their talents. They were often misplaced; for instance, one who studied engineering ended up as a teacher in a primary school.

Mohamed Ali was adamant about what he wanted those students to take from the West. He had no interest in European political ideas or in skills that would not serve his military goals. His whole educational policy was designed to serve his military as well as to produce state employees. Missions abroad were under strict control and surveillance; he received and read reports of the progress of his students. When he learned that one of them had given up his traditional attire and wore British clothes, he wrote him angrily saying he had not sent him to take up European dress. Students were discouraged from travelling in their host countries.

Two large missions were sent in 1844 and 1847. Together and with students who had been sent individually, they compromised 169 students. These missions were significant for including two of Mohamed Ali's sons and two of his grandchildren, one of whom, Ismail, would become the future ruler of Egypt. They also included a number of future leading politicians and civil servants such as Sherif Pasha and Nubar Pasha who would both rise to be prime ministers and Ali Mubarak who would be instrumental in organizing Egyptian education. Unlike with earlier missions, European influence on the students' hearts and minds is clearly traceable. Whether Mohamed Ali liked it or not, European ideas were beginning to spread among the students who would form the new emerging elite.

The man who exemplified the change the most was Rifa'a El Tahtawi (1801–1873). Rifaa had studied in Al Azhar under his mentor Sheikh Hassan El Attar. Attar, whom we met earlier visiting the French scientists during the invasion, played a key role in Tahtawi's life. He was clearly aware of the huge gap that existed between Egypt and Europe and argued that conditions in Egypt must change. He first recommended Tahtawi as chaplain of a military unit and then in 1826 as imam to the mission sent to Paris. Ironically it was Tahtawi and not any of the students in that mission who would achieve the greatest fame. Intellectually curious, he was not content with merely being the mission's imam but instead studied and interacted mostly with his French hosts. Responsible for a variety of educational projects after his return, he was also a translator of numerous books. His most famous work, however, was the memoir he wrote reflecting on his five years in France.

One author who left a significant impact on Tahtawi was Montesquieu. From him, he borrowed the idea of love to one's country as the foundation of civic duty. Tahtawi formulated the first attempt to clarify what it meant to be an Egyptian. He was clearly influenced by the European interest in ancient Egypt and encouraged pride in Egypt's history. French qualities that impressed him the most, as evident from his book, were cleanliness, intellectual curiosity, and the French hatred of laziness. Although Tahtawi was influenced by his stay in France, many of his basic conceptions did not change. The ideal ruler for him was the man who had sent him to France, Mohamed Ali, a ruler who enacted reforms yet remained traditional. Non-Muslims were to be treated nicely, but they were not viewed as equal. He continued to see them in traditional terms as protected *dhimmi* people.

One significant argument that Tahtawi developed was his defense of the adoption of modern sciences. Tahtawi argued that these were not alien to Muslims. Centuries earlier, Muslims had built a great civilization and had made important scientific discoveries. Science was once Islamic. Muslims had entered a dark age when they neglected the sciences, but now they could borrow them back from the Europeans. This line of argument is still used today. It contained two important premises that formed the center of how modernity was viewed. First, in stating that sciences were Islamic,[5] an argument was being made that there was nothing fundamentally wrong with Islam or Muslims. True, they had fallen through a dark age, but they had been great once before. They were, in fact, the founders of science. Secondly, science was thus understood as a set of technical devices. No comprehension is evident of modernity as a clear break in the history of man.

By 1841, Mohamed Ali's project had run its full course. Faced with a unified European military campaign, he was forced to withdraw his forces from Turkey, Greater Syria, and Arabia. In peacetime, the new rules stipulated that the Egyptian army was not to exceed eighteen thousand men. In return, Mohamed Ali had secured hereditary rule of Egypt for his family. With no need for the new industries and schools to supply the military, they were soon closed one after the other. When Mohamed Ali died in 1849 he was followed by his grandson Abbas I (1812–1854). Abbas, described by historians as a pure Turk, is often blamed by contemporary Egyptians for ending the modernization project. He disliked foreigners, especially the French, and is recorded as having

---

5. The expression commonly used by future writers is: "This is our merchandise being returned to us."

attempted to banish all Copts from Egypt to the Sudan, only to be stopped by the intervention of the sheikh of Al Azhar. In reality, however, there was never a modernization project to begin with. What Egypt had witnessed had been a short-lived attempt to build a modern army and that had come to an end before Abbas succeeded his grandfather. True, forty-one students were sent abroad under Abbas, but those were the last glimpses of a dream.

Notwithstanding the short-term nature of the project, it did leave its imprint on the future development of Egypt. From the moment of its conception, the project was the dream of one man. By virtue of being ruler, that man was fortunate enough to implement his plan, but nevertheless it remained a single man's scheme. No intellectual awakening similar to the one in Europe preceded or accompanied the reforms Mohamed Ali introduced. A despot had decided the course the country was to follow and imposed his will on a reluctant population. His reforms, especially forced conscription were met with resentment and sometimes open revolt.

Mohamed Ali succeeded in creating a new class of civil servants. It included Turks, Armenians, and other foreigners but, along the way, also an increasing number of Egyptians. What he did not create however was an independent bourgeoisie. This would have to wait for his grandson Ismail. This lack of an independent bourgeoisie would have a profound impact on the future development of liberalism in Egypt and the shape it took. Egyptian liberalism would emerge not from an independent bourgeoisie but from civil servants, men whose lives were tied to the state and whose conceptions were inherently shaped by that. With no tension between the individual and the state, Egyptian liberals' ultimate dream would be a repetition of the story of Mohamed Ali, an autocrat imposing reforms from above on a reluctant population.

Mohamed Ali enjoyed having the lives of great men translated and read to him. Perhaps he saw himself in their stories. It is claimed that one of his secretaries came up with the idea of translating Machiavelli's *The Prince* for him. For three days, the translated part was read to him. On the fourth day, Mohamed Ali reportedly informed the translator that he did not want him to continue. He told him: "I have nothing to learn from Machiavelli. I know more tricks than he knew."

A Minority Like No Other

But where were Copts during all those changes? Weren't they part of the story? Mohamed Ali had found Copts in the same state that they had been living in for centuries. In certain respects he continued the familiar patterns of the ruler-Copts relationship. More than once, Mohamed Ali arrested Coptic civil servants and levied sums of money on them. Guirguis El Gohary was the leading Coptic civil servant and Mohamed Ali extorted his money from him. Mohamed Ali elevated Moalem Ghali to prominence only to order him killed in 1822 to be succeeded by his son Moalem Basilious. Similarly in 1817, Mohamed Ali re-imposed the dress codes on Copts barring them from wearing white turbans, in the last instance of dress codes being imposed in Egypt. He also encouraged conversion to Islam by granting those who converted financial rewards, though no force was used. The testimony of Christians, even foreigners, was never taken against a Muslim. Even Clot Bey, who headed the medical administration of the country, was not allowed to testify against a Muslim student who had physically attacked him. The student was nevertheless punished. Mohamed Ali broke the power of Coptic civil servants by replacing them with Syrians and Armenians. That move was driven not by a sectarian agenda but rather the replacement of old elements with newer more modern ones, similar to his destruction of the power of the Mamluks and sheikhs.

On the other hand, Mohamed Ali was much more tolerant toward Copts than any of his predecessors. He granted approvals to church renovation requests and allowed Copts to go on pilgrimage to the Holy Land. Although he depended on foreigners, especially Armenians, as his chief secretaries and ministers, he elevated some Copts as city mayors which was unprecedented in Egypt. He also granted Basilius Ghali the title of bey making him the first Copt to be elevated to this rank. His most important intervention for Copts came after the martyrdom of Sidhom Bishay in Damietta. Sidhom had been accused of insulting Islam and after a hasty trial was found guilty and ordered flogged. After the flogging, the mob took him and beat him through the city streets. He died five days later from his wounds. The foreign consuls in Damietta raised the issue to Moahmed Ali who ordered a reinvestigation. The investigation implicated the governor and judge in the death. Mohamed Ali ordered both removed from their positions and banished. He furthermore allowed Copts for the first time to raise crosses in their funerals.

Histories written by Copts record a number of friendly encounters between Mohamed Ali and the Coptic pope. Mohamed Ali's daughter had reportedly been sick and a bishop cast a demon from her. In another instance, Mohamed Ali's son, Ibrahim Pasha questioned the authenticity of the Holy Fire that appears every year in the Church of Holy Sepulcher. He accompanied the Coptic pope and Greek Orthodox patriarch of Jerusalem inside the tomb. The Holy Fire appeared in front of a frightened Ibrahim. Regardless of the truthfulness of those stories, they reflect Copts' friendly view of Mohamed Ali as a ruler.

As Egypt's largest Christian community, Copts attracted the interests of the great powers. Tsarist Russia, which took upon its shoulders the protection of the Orthodox communities in the Ottoman Empire, attempted to do the same for Copts. A Russian emissary is recorded by Coptic historians as being sent to meet with the Coptic Pope Peter VII (r. 1809–1852) and offer him protection. Copts from now on were to be under the protection of the tsar, he declared to the aging pope. The pope looked at him and asked him whether his tsar died? The bewildered emissary replied affirmatively. The tsar was human and died like all other men. The pope smiled and asked him: "Why should I seek protection from one who dies, when we are under the protection of the Living that never dies?" Unlike other minorities, Copts never accepted foreign protection.

Mohamed Ali's invasion of Sudan allowed Pope Peter VII to consecrate bishops for the Christians there for the first time in centuries. Trouble however brewed in Ethiopia. Under the influence of foreign missionaries and military advisors, the relationship between the mother and daughter churches was showing signs of strain. After Pope Peter VII's letters to the Ethiopian emperor failed to solve the matter, he sent a delegation to Ethiopia to deal with the roots of the conflict. The delegation was headed by the brilliant monk Daoud Al Antony who would later succeed him to the papal throne.

The greatest challenge to the community, however, was continued Catholic and Protestant attempts to convert Copts. Mohamed Ali, who was told such a move would help his relations with Europe, asked Moalem Ghali to convert to Catholicism, which he did with his family. This conversion gave the Catholic church its largest group of followers in Egypt and would eventually lead to the establishment of the Coptic Catholic Church which would follow the pope in Rome while retaining its Eastern Coptic rituals.

The missionaries' work gained further momentum under Mohamed Ali. Encouraged by the increasing number of foreigners employed in Egypt, Catholic missionaries were able to open two schools in Alexandria and one for girls in Cairo. A Protestant school was also opened in Cairo. Together they proved attractive to Copts who were seeking a better education and future. Coptic priests accused the teachers of proselytizing and attempting to convert the students. With no modern schools of their own, Copts could hardly compete. The church lamented for its followers. It had tended the sheep Christ had given it throughout the centuries and paid for their faith to be kept alive with blood and suddenly the Catholics and Protestants were stealing them away. The Coptic Church had suffered and toiled for hundreds of years, while now others reaped the fruits of its labor.

The challenge of course went much deeper than mere education. True, the church had managed to survive for centuries against overwhelming odds, but the quality of its teaching had been affected in the process. Priests could hardly read and write and often just memorized and recited prayers they could not understand. A few scholars appeared in each century and defended what it meant to be Orthodox but they were becoming scarce. The church was facing the onslaught of missionaries and at its disposal were few weapons to defend itself and its teachings. The task was colossal but it would soon find its worthy man. The monk who was sent to Ethiopia would soon return, and he would soon be called Kyrillos IV, the father of reform.

CHAPTER FOUR

What Is Modernity Anyway?

The Follies of Said

THE YEAR 1854 WAS A WATERSHED MOMENT, both in Egyptian history and for the Coptic Church. The assassination of Abbas that year ended what is often described as a dark period in Egyptian history and brought Mohamed Said Pasha, Mohamed Ali's son, to the governorship of Egypt.[1] Simultaneously, after a two-year delay, the struggle inside the Coptic Church was resolved and Kyrillos IV was finally enthroned as Coptic pope. While both men were strikingly different from their predecessors, they were also quite dissimilar in how they viewed the challenges that modernity posed.

In the years leading up to his assassination by his Mamluks, Abbas had grown distant from his family. Most of them had left Egypt for Istanbul where they were involved in conspiracies against him with some accused of having a hand in his murder. His assassination opened the door not only for his uncle, Said, to become the ruler of Egypt, but for the rest of the family to return

---

1. According to Ottoman customs and laws, the governorship of Egypt, while remaining in the Mohamed Ali family, would pass not from father to son, but to the eldest family member. Thus, Mohamed Ali was succeeded by his grandson Abbas (b. 1812) before his own son Said (b. 1822).

and take part in both government and managing the huge inheritance Mohamed Ali had left them. Said was completely different from his nephew in disposition. Unlike Abbas, who disliked foreigners and kept them as far away as possible, Said felt most comfortable with them, especially the French. Said had been educated by European tutors, who had clearly influenced his inclinations. He spoke good English and French but could not even write Turkish.

Throughout his rule, Said was surrounded by Europeans, mostly adventurers who sought to milk as much money from him as they could. A committed Francophone, he signed onto the Suez Canal project that his friend, the former French diplomat Ferdinand-Marie de Lesseps sold him. This agreement would have profound implications for Egypt's future. Not only were the agreement's articles unfavorable to Egypt, but the moment the Suez Canal materialized from a dream into a reality, the fate of Egypt became central to British interests. It became integral to their policy towards the jewel of their empire: India.

Said's obsession throughout his rule was his image in the eyes of Europeans. A man of weak character, he fell in love with Europe and what mattered most to him was how Europeans viewed him. He wished to be remembered by history and Europeans—the two not quite distinct for him—as a benevolent and liberal ruler. This fixation on his image led to deliberate attempts to appear tolerant, modern, and Western, different from the image of the normal Eastern ruler at the time. It is perhaps the word "image" that best describes his passion. For him, modernity, if he ever thought of the term, was to copy, not European technologies as his father had attempted, not the foundations of European thought, but their manifestations in appearances. A prime example was his passion for the army. His army did not obtain new weapons or better trainers. It received new clothes modeled on the latest fashions of

Europe and endless drills and marches to European music. His attempt to appear and be remembered as a modern enlightened ruler meant the adoption of the outer layers of what he perceived as civilization, but hardly anything deeper. Schools were opened, and then closed; others were merged then separated once again, and civil servants were replaced constantly leaving no possibility for the adoption of any coherent policy.

This need to impress Europeans meant the rise of the influence of consuls who were able to exploit Said's character to the benefit of their citizens. Not only did Said buy into all sorts of projects that were presented to him, but he also was forced to pay huge sums of money to Europeans in exchange for abandoning those very projects or as indemnity for losses, real or imagined. While during his first years as governor he benefited from high grain prices which led to economic prosperity, by the end of his rule Egypt's financial situation was showing signs of serious troubles.

Unlike his two predecessors, Said viewed himself not as a Turk but as an Egyptian. Later on, Ahmed Orabi would remember Said's years fondly as the years Egyptian officers received huge promotions in the army. He would also point to a speech Said gave in which he stated that he was an Egyptian and articulated his dreams for the country. Speeches were followed by actual policies. The Arabization of the government took place in 1857. These policies, especially the ones affecting the army, alienated Turkish and Circassian officers.

Said's rule saw the emancipation of Copts from the last legal restrictions of dhimmitude, though not their social ramifications. In December 1855, the *jizya* was finally abolished. A month later, in January 1856, Said ordered the conscription of Christians into the army. This move was not entirely welcomed by Copts however. At the time, conscription was viewed unfavorably by the peasant population, be it Christian or Muslim, as it meant years of military service away from their families and their lands. Copts' resentment of conscription was also due to perceived attempts within the army at forced conversion to Islam. Soon, Said abandoned the attempt. Copts would not be fully conscripted until the reign of Khedive Ismail. Said also ordered the cancellation of celebrations that were held whenever a Copt converted to Islam. Furthermore, unlike his nephew, Said permitted the building of new churches and the renovation of old ones. He sent the first Copt[2] in one of the student missions to France, and appointed an Armenian Christian as governor of Sudan.

These unprecedented moves require explanation. Some have opted to view them as part of a continuous pattern since the days of Mohamed Ali. Thus Mohamed Ali's re-imposition of the dress code in 1817 was the last time for those discriminatory laws and the legal framework of dhimmitude was removed step by step. Others have pointed to Said's character and his fixation on appearing as a modern and liberal ruler as the explanation of those steps. It is important to note however that while traditional Egyptian historiography has dealt with Egypt as completely separate from the Ottoman Empire since 1805, and while Egypt's rulers did indeed enjoy tremendous freedom of action, Egypt was still, at least legally, part of the Ottoman Empire. More importantly, the ties between Egypt's rulers and the empire remained. Said, Ismail, and the rest of their family members found refuge in Istanbul during Abbas's reign. Similarly, Ismail's brother Mustafa Fazl and his uncle Mohamed Abdel Halim moved to Istanbul after Ismail managed to change the rules of succession. Nor were the ties merely geographic, members of the Egyptian royal family in Istanbul

---

2. Most historians agree that the first Copt sent was Azmy Wassef during Said's reign. Iris Habib El Masry dissents from this view and identifies Ibrahim El Sobki who was sent by Mohamed Ali in 1847 as the first Copt in an education mission. The name Ibrahim El Sobki can go both ways.

occupied important positions with Prince Mohamed Said Halim becoming grand vizier in 1913. Said's view of himself as an Egyptian was the outlier not the norm. The ruling class in Egypt, whether the members of the royal family themselves or the highest level civil servants, were Turks and continued to view themselves as such. It is thus important to note that Said's moves coincided with similar ones in the Ottoman Empire. On February 18, 1856, Sultan Abdel Mejid I issued extensive reforms called the *Khat El Hamayuni.** Promising equality for all citizens of the empire regardless of religion, those reforms aimed to eliminate all forms of arbitrary discrimination at the local level throughout the empire. The Articles in the decree would have profound future implications for Copts in relation to the building of new churches.

A VOICE CRYING IN THE WILDERNESS?

Kyrillos IV was born Daoud (David) in 1816 to a poor illiterate family. In 1838, at twenty-two years of age, he left the world to become a monk at St. Anthony's Monastery in the Eastern Desert. In an extraordinary move, he was chosen as the monastery's abbot only two years after his ordination as a monk. By that time, he had already shown signs of his exceptional mind and talents. As abbot, he was responsible for the monastery's land endowments in Beni Suef. There he started a school and established a library. These initiatives were quite unusual at the time and showed a mind concerned with education and knowledge.

Having built a reputation for himself as a reformer, he was put forward as a candidate for the papacy while still in Ethiopia upon the death of Pope Peter VII. While historians agree that his

* Ottoman Reform Edict

candidacy was met with refusal by some Copts and that a struggle ensued, it remains unclear what the conflict was about. We are told that those opposed to his candidacy preferred elevating the bishop of Akhmim to the papacy. Those against Daoud's nomination attempted to involve the state in the dispute. They even attempted to consecrate their candidate secretly, but were stopped violently by Daoud's supporters. Abbas, who believed in superstitions, was told that the consecration of Daoud would mean the end of his own life and thus refused to allow it. In 1853, however, Abbas was convinced to allow Daoud's consecration as auxiliary bishop responsible for the affairs of the church. As such, he immediately embarked on his program of reform by establishing the first modern Coptic school in 1854. By June 1854, those against him had been swayed, and Abbas allowed him to be consecrated pope. Remarkably, Abbas was assassinated a month later.

Though Pope Kyrillos IV reigned for only seven years, he accomplished what in retrospect seems like the work of decades. His first focus was on education and he established a total of five modern schools. Two of these were for girls making them the first Egyptian girls' schools in the modern age. Besides the sciences, the curriculum of these schools included six languages, one of which was Coptic. It is due to his efforts that the Coptic language was resurrected. He also made sure to teach Coptic students the old Coptic hymns, saving them from eternal loss. Pope Kyrillos IV took personal interest in his schools urging foreigners to pay them a visit and judge the quality of the education they provided. Most remarkable is that he opened his schools to all students regardless of creed. Given that education was provided for free, from the papacy's own finances, such a move was astonishing at the time.

The second area that grabbed his attention was printing. He ordered a printing press from Europe and, in preparation for its arrival, arranged for four Copts to be trained at the government press. When the printing press arrived in Alexandria, he ordered the priests and deacons to welcome it in a march with hymns and the reciting of the psalms. When informed that such an action raised people's eyebrows he proclaimed: "I am not honoring a machine made of iron. I am honoring the knowledge that will be spread through it." Furthermore, he established the Patriarchal Library in Cairo.

Thirdly, he paid special attention to the organization of the church. He reorganized the church endowments and established an office in the papacy to handle their management and the financial affairs of the church. In Cairo, priests gathered each week for discussions in order to elevate their knowledge of the scripture. He also attempted, unsuccessfully, to provide priests with fixed salaries to stop the practice of receiving financial compensation for religious services. Additionally, he began construction of a new cathedral as the seat of the papacy. He paid special attention to women not only in terms of education, but also took steps to deal with social ills that had taken hold in the previous centuries. He forbade marriages to girls under the age of fourteen and attempted to give females inheritance rights equal to those of males.

Naturally, such aggressive efforts at reform were met with opposition by various sectors of the Coptic community. Scribes tried to incite the people against the printing press as it meant an end to their source of living. Traditional teachers in the old Coptic *kuttabs* incited parents against the new schools which led to many parents refusing to send their children there. Pope Kyrillos IV was accused of squandering the church finances with his reform program.

Kyrillos IV was not only a reformer within the church, but also a defender of Copts in general. He is said to have met Said and put forward three Coptic demands: admission to the higher government schools, membership in the local councils, and equal opportunity to jobs in the civil service. Said stalled and these demands on behalf of Copts are often cited as one of the reasons for Kyrillos's supposed murder by poison, supposedly on Said's orders. Another possible contribution to his murder was his perceived attempt to achieve church unity. Kyrillos was thought to harbor dreams of uniting the Orthodox churches and ending their centuries-old division. His closeness to the Armenian bishop and Eastern Orthodox patriarch gave further credence to the rumors. Kyrillos IV had also played the traditional role his predecessors had as diplomat to Ethiopia, having been sent there as Said's emissary.

What explains such a tremendous program of reform? The most remarkable aspect of Kyrillos's reforms is that they were unprecedented. History does not record any such measures by his predecessors nor of any of his contemporaries among the bishops and priests. Kyrillos seemed to invent his reforms out of thin air and enact them without any previous foundation. After his death, his much celebrated printing press was left to decay, but his educational policy left its mark. His schools were instrumental in educating not only Coptic youth but also Muslims. To be able to fully understand their future impact, one has only to realize that four of Egypt's future prime ministers, two Copts and two Muslims, received their education at his Coptic schools.

Some historians have attributed his reforms to the Protestant Church Missionary Society. Unlike later Protestant missionaries, they did not aim to convert Copts but only to help the existing Coptic Church. They viewed the Coptic Church as essentially a sound church that had decayed and deteriorated over the years; it only needed a helping hand to stand on its feet once again. Their work was focused on distributing Bibles, establishing a school, and holding Christian meetings in order to lead Copts back to the purity of the scripture and thus cleanse the church from its diseases internally.

One early account claimed that Kyrillos had been a student in the Protestant missionaries' school, a claim that holds no truth. If Kyrillos IV had been their student, they would certainly have celebrated that fact in their correspondence with their headquarters in Britain. It is true that the Church Missionary Society's priest, John Lieder, was close to Kyrillos and probably influenced his ideas, but Kyrillos's reformist mindset goes back to his time as abbot of St. Anthony's Monastery, well before he had any contact with the missionaries. Whatever the source of his reforms, whether they were developed on his own, upon the suggestion of foreigners, or a combination of both, they presented the first serious attempt to answer the challenges posed by modernity.

"My Country Is No Longer in Africa. It is in Europe."

The death of Said ushered Khedive Ismail into the governorship of Egypt. If Said was obsessed with his image in the eyes of Europeans, Ismail took that obsession to a whole new level. Educated in Europe as part of Mohamed Ali's 1844 mission, Ismail was Egypt's first completely Westernized ruler. Ismail was clearly bedazzled by Europe but his enchantment was of a peculiar nature. It was the outer manifestations of civilization that grabbed his attention. He seemed convinced that by copying the details, style, and appearances of Europe, Egypt would be transformed to becoming part of it. In a sense, this betrayed a fundamental lack of understanding not only of the road Europe had taken to become what it was, but also of the clear differences between Europe and Egypt and thus the obstacles an attempt at imitation would face. He failed completely to build lasting institutions that would support the changes he implemented. Like his grandfather, Mohamed Ali, he succeeded in further breaking traditional modes of social organization but, like him, fared quite poorly in building lasting ones.

His copying of the appearance instead of the spirit of Western civilization took various forms. First Ismail insisted on imitating the manner and style of European courts. Welcoming foreign counselors for the first time, he asked Nubar to write him a speech which he gave blindly, not realizing the promises Nubar had written into it. He embarked on an impressive program of grand projects not least of which was an opera house. The adoption of European appearances also took the form of sponsorship of the arts, the establishment of a museum, a Geographical Society, and copying building styles. His lavish spending on the opening of the Suez Canal was to a large extent an attempt to be accepted as an equal by European monarchs.

Perhaps the most bizarre part of the obsession with imitating Europe was in his adventures in Africa. Convinced that to become part of Europe, Egypt needed an empire in Africa, he entered into a war with Ethiopia that proved both costly and ultimately worthless. He famously declared: "My country is no longer in Africa. It is in Europe." No statement better embodies the follies of the man and his dreams.

Ismail's spending spree was not limited to Western buildings and style. In order to change the rules of governance of Egypt so that his sons could rule after him, he spent a huge sum of money to bribe Ottoman officials.[3] To change the humiliating provisions of the Suez Canal agreement his predecessor had signed, he appealed to Emperor Napoleon III and agreed to pay the huge sum of money that the ruling entailed. Initially Ismail benefited from the huge increase in cotton prices due to the American Civil

---

3. Ismail succeeded in changing the inheritance rules for the governorship of Egypt from the oldest member of the Mohamed Ali family to inheritance from father to son.

War, but once that war ended and American cotton production recovered, Egypt's revenues could not keep up with his spending and he was forced to seek loans from foreign creditors. Those loans would ultimately lead to his downfall.

It was during Ismail's reign that education was finally separated from military affairs. An explosion of both government and private schools would open the door for the birth of a new generation that would shape Egypt's future. By 1878, European schools in Egypt had more than twelve thousand students including more than a thousand Egyptian Muslims. In January 1873 Ismail opened the first government girls' school, and, by 1875, modern government schools had nearly five thousand students. Two important developments deserve noting. First, the duality of religious vs. modern education was created during this period. Compared to the five thousand students in modern government schools, there were one hundred twelve thousand students in religious *kuttabs*. While in 1867 the government took control of the rich *kuttabs*, the nature of Egyptian education as two separate entities was established. Even in those *kuttabs* taken over by the government, education was quite weak with teachers incapable of teaching arithmetic. In the modern government schools, the teaching of Arabic and religion remained the domain of sheikhs. Out of 366 teachers employed by the government in 1875, 127 were sheikhs. No attempt was made to modernize teaching methods of Arabic or touch the way religion was taught. This would have to await the reforming efforts of Mohamed Abdu later on.

Secondly, while separated from military affairs in terms of management, the government's educational policy was tailored to produce military and civil service employees. Between 1865 and 1875, a full 63 percent of graduates from modern government schools took jobs in the army with another 19 percent entering the civil service. The rise of the new educated class that had benefited from Mohamed Ali's policies did not mean their separation from the state. The men who had been formed in the service of the state could not break from that relationship. A prime example was Ali Mubarak, who had been a student with Ismail in the 1844 mission. Managing Egypt's educational policy, the reforms he introduced were however limited in nature. His reforms were achieved within the limits of what Ismail allowed.

The state remained the initiator of the modernization project and government service remained the ultimate dream of the emerging educated Egyptians. Their understanding of modernization would for a very long time be tied to their conception of the state. Their ultimate dream would continue being a Mohamed Ali or an Ismail who would compel an "ignorant population" to modernize. It was thus inevitable that these "emerging liberals" would never develop any interest in speaking to their fellow Egyptians, but instead would be focused on convincing the ruler of their modernizing projects. Their "liberalism" was inherently illiberal.

It is also important to note the huge influence that France and French ideas had on these "emerging liberals." The adoption of the French legal code meant that generations of Egyptian lawyers and judges looked up to France as the source of learning. France had been an important source of advisors and trainers for Mohamed Ali and this continued under Ismail. It also remained the preferred destination for student missions sent by the Egyptian state. French schools were widespread in Egypt with the number of students in French schools under the British occupation reaching 24,000 students compared to 3,300 students in British schools. After the British occupation, Egyptian nationals continued to look to France as a source of inspiration and support in their nationalist aspirations for independence and were thus enchanted with the French model. This would have profound implications for the nature of the liberalism adopted especially in regards to the understanding of secularism.

During Ismail's reign, Egyptians were exposed to Europeans and European ideas more than ever before. From a mere 3,000 in 1836, Egypt's European population reached 79,000 in 1871. The growth of the foreign population continued under the British occupation reaching 260,000 in 1917. The largest European communities were Greeks and Italians followed by the French and British. While Europeans represented around 2 percent of the population, they were heavily concentrated in cities. Cairo's inhabitants were 9 percent European, with Suez at 14 percent and Alexandria 20 percent. The daily contact with and exposure to Europeans left its mark on the formation of Egyptian political ideas as well as social habits.

The increase in European inhabitants in Egypt led not only to a dramatic increase in European schools but also to the emergence of an independent press. Ismail, keen to impress Europeans, financed foreign language newspapers with the aim of painting a favorable picture of his rule. Newspapers however were not only a government domain. Independent European newspapers to serve the growing European community emerged and in time, independent Egyptian newspapers. The pioneers in that field were largely Syrian immigrants in Egypt. By 1877, there were opposition newspapers in Egypt that attacked Ismail's policies ferociously. While the first anti-Ismail sentiments were championed by non-Egyptians such as Gamal El Din El Afghani, Yacoub Sanou' and Selim El Nakkash, the events that would ultimately lead to Ismail's fall led more and more Egyptians to become involved.

Ismail is considered the first ruler who was friendly to Christians. Such a reputation appears to be deserved. He appointed Copts as judges in Egyptian courts for the first time as well as giving them equal rights in political participation and representation in the first Assembly of Delegates in 1866. He allowed churches to be built even in such cities as Tanta, which were viewed as exclusively Islamic. Copts were accepted equally in government schools and numerous Copts were sent in the student missions to Europe. During Ismail's reign, the first non-Muslim, Nubar, an Armenian, became a pasha. While Nubar was not a Copt, the move was still hailed in opening the door to non-Muslims to reach the highest offices of government and honor. Furthermore, Ismail gave financial contributions to Coptic schools as well as European missionary ones. In cases of conversion to Islam, Ismail ordered that the person converting must be given an audience with a priest who would debate him on his decision before such a conversion became legal. This practice, which became known as "Sessions of Advice and Guidance," helped make sure that coercion was not used. It would continue, largely uninterrupted, until the last years of Hosni Mubarak's rule.

However, the most significant development during Ismail's reign was the development of private land ownership. Mohamed Ali had given huge tracts of uncultivated lands to his family before he died. In 1858, Said further upheld the right of inheritance of those lands. However it was under Ismail that this would be recognized as private property with all the rights that would entail. In 1871, due to the dire state of the country's finances, Ismail proposed a private property land law, whereby the payment of six times the annual tax in one installment would entail complete ownership as well as a reduction by half of future taxes. While driven by financial needs, and ultimately not beneficial to the state's finances, the new law ushered in a monumental change in Egypt, the birth of an independent, landed bourgeoisie. Ismail further distributed tracts of land to various state employees. The forced selling of his own land in order to meet the financial crisis in his last years as well as under the British occupation in 1885 would further speed the process.

The beginnings of political participation by Egyptians started uneventfully. In 1866, as part of his attempt to transform Egypt into a European country, Ismail ordered the establishment of an Assembly of Delegates. At that moment there was no popular demand for political participation; instead it was merely the act of a ruler. In its first session, the delegates were informed that they should sit according to their political affiliations; those supporting the government on the right side of the chamber, those against it on the left and those in the middle should sit at the center. All the delegates immediately moved to the right declaring that "we cannot be opposed to the khedive's government." A number of developments led that unimpressive elected body to become a serious medium of not only debate but action.

Ismail had led the country to near financial collapse. His excessive borrowing, at unfavorable interest rates, led to the accumulation of a huge debt that the country could not repay. As a result, he began to take measures to cut government expenditure and raise taxes. These measures naturally affected the new landed bourgeoisie who comprised the absolute majority of the delegates. As in the case of the American Revolution, higher taxation led to a call for representation. The assembly was no longer content to sit on the right nodding approvingly at every government policy, but insisted on examining and criticizing those policies.

Ismail's debt crisis and his attempt to escape his financial obligations to his creditors led European governments to interfere on behalf of their citizens. They forced Ismail to give up his chairmanship of the cabinet and appoint Nubar Pasha as the first prime minister. Nubar's ministry included two Europeans, one French and one British, to oversee Egypt's finances and government spending. The weakening of Ismail's power by European powers gave room for the new emerging class to play a role in their country's future. But more importantly, the appointment of two European ministers fueled public anger and resentment. Ismail further tried to incite the population against foreign intervention. He attempted to use the press, the Assembly of Delegates and public opinion in general against his creditors and the European powers. Foreign intervention in the internal affairs of the country coincided with the birth of the constitutional movement in Egypt which would have profound effects on its future development. It would ultimately lead to a love-hate relationship with the West as a source of inspiration and a model of modernity and, at the same time, the hated occupier. Egyptian liberalism would never escape this dichotomy.

In the end, Ismail was playing a game in which he had no winning cards. His fate was sealed when the European powers secured an order from the Ottoman Sultan removing him from the governorship of Egypt. His son Khedive Tawfik replaced him in 1879 and Ismail was forced into exile. His grandiose dreams came crashing down and with them the fate of the whole country. In 1875 he was forced to sell Egypt's shares in the Suez Canal. For a small amount of money, the British Prime Minister Disraeli bought those shares, and with them a stake in the Egypt's future.

Ismail introduced enormous changes in Egyptian society. The Egyptian landed bourgeoisie was born during his reign. He introduced constitutionalism to Egypt, and his reign witnessed the birth of an independent press, a growth in education, and increased contact with Europeans. Dreaming of making Egypt part of Europe, he largely succeeded though not in the way he intended. As a historian of modern Egypt remarked, after all, his policies brought European occupation to Egypt in 1882.

REVIVAL VS. REFORM: WHO LEADS THE CHURCH?

As Egypt was formulating its understanding of modernity and attempting to develop answers to the challenges it posed, the Coptic community led by the church was facing its own crisis of modernity. Little had changed in the preceding centuries in the church's mode of operation and its teachings. Modernity was accompanied by the onslaught of foreign missionaries, and while the church throughout the centuries had developed answers and rebuttals to Catholic challenges, Protestantism was a completely new competitor. Similarly, the removal of the legal framework of dhimittude opened the Coptic community to both new opportunities and challenges. The church found itself ill-equipped to deal with changing circumstances.

Kyrillos IV had attempted to answer those challenges by adopting a dual policy: reorganizing the church through his various administrative initiatives as well as introducing modern education for the benefit of the community at large. While both seemed compatible at the time, the two approaches inevitably led to a clash between the clergy and the laity. The administrative reforms would eventually lead to the development of a centralized church hierarchy that naturally viewed itself as the true guardians of the community and its emerging identity. On the other hand, the introduction of modern education gave birth to a new generation of Copts who due to that very education viewed themselves as the true representatives of the community and the ones best equipped to manage its affairs. Furthermore, the two approaches were not undertaken in a vacuum. Like their fellow countrymen, Copts were affected, both as a church and as a community, by the answers the Egyptian state and ultimately the new emerging Egyptian elite found to meet the challenges of modernity. In the long run, urbanization, especially immigration to Cairo, meant the strengthening of the pope's hand in the face of local bishops, while the rise of the new Egyptian elite, part of whom were Copts, in the service of the state meant not only their increased awareness and dissatisfaction with the church's conditions but also their increased ability to put their concerns into actions and use the state's power in internal Coptic disputes. The old mode of operation was falling apart and the clergy and the new Coptic elite were locked in a competition on shaping a new one.

The clash between clergy and laity was not in itself new. Unlike the Catholic approach, the laity had always played a significant role in the affairs of the Coptic Orthodox Church. The Coptic laity had always taken part in choosing the new pope. Partly this was due to centuries under Muslim rule, during which Coptic civil servants became powerful representatives of the community and attempted in turn to influence decision making in the church. But, more importantly, it was due to the specific Orthodox view of the role of the clergy and laity. At various moments in church history, the clergy and laity found themselves engaged in a struggle of control over church affairs and the Coptic community at large. The modern struggle between clergy and the Coptic elite however was novel in both the new issues in contention between them, and the new opportunities and methods each side employed in their struggle. The clash would reach its climax under Kyrillos V (r. 1874–1927) leading to his banishment and triumphant return.

In between the two Kyrilloses was the papacy of Demetrius II (r. 1861–1870). Unlike his reforming predecessor, Pope Demetrius launched no new reform initiatives. While the schools his predecessor had established continued and increased in number, the quality of their education deteriorated. The printing press that Kyrillos IV had so eagerly awaited went unused and was lent to a family that used it to print religious books and, ultimately, to publish the Coptic *El Watan* newspaper. Some have attributed Demetrius's approach to a warning not to follow in his predecessor's steps that he received from Said upon becoming pope. Certainly, rumors of Kyrillos's poisoning at the hands of Said did not encourage the new pope to institute reforms. His efforts during his papacy were focused on fighting the emerging Protestant threat.

Unlike the previous Church Missionary Society, new missionaries in Egypt led by the American United Presbyterian Mission, did not view the Coptic Church favorably. For them, the Coptic Church, with its ancient traditions and theological views, was a dead church and beyond redemption. Only by converting Copts was there any hope for their salvation. The new missionaries began in earnest in the late 1850s after the 1850 Ottoman recognition of Protestants as a separate entity in the empire. Missions arrived in Egypt in 1854, 1856, 1858, 1860, and 1861. By 1865 they had reached Asyut, which became a center for their activities and the major area of their success.

The missionaries' success was in a sense inevitable. The ancient Coptic Church with its uneducated clergy was ill-equipped to meet the challenge. Whatever theological strength the Coptic Church had in its early years, the fire of Alexandrian theology had dwindled. Christian practices were performed more out of habit. The missionaries brought with them new preaching techniques. Their service was purely in Arabic, which was appealing to a community that had lost its ancient Coptic language. An Arab translation of the Bible was published in 1864 and the missionaries began spreading this edition among Copts. Their services were livelier and brought a personal message of salvation. They brought their message into Coptic homes, which was unprecedented.

Besides its religious appeal, joining the Protestant Church had material benefits. Protestant missionaries opened modern schools that offered their students a better future. The first Protestant school opened by those new missionaries was established in 1855. By 1870 there were twelve of them with 633 students. The growth continued, reaching 168 schools with 11,014 students in 1897. The Protestants established hospitals and orphanages and, by 1914, began Sunday schools. Some of the first to convert were the counselors for foreign governments in various cities in Egypt. Many rich Copts in the south had established connections with Western countries and, more than Muslims, became their counselors in Egypt. Gindy Wissa became counselor for Italy, Beshara Ebeid for France, Wissa Boctor and Wassef Khayat for the United States. All those men and their families converted to Protestantism. While there may not have been direct causation, there was certainly a correlation between their occupation as counselors and their conversion.

The attack on the Coptic Church's traditions and theology was mounting. It even reached the level of physical attacks, with three converts to Protestantism trying to burn a church in Asyut as early as 1865 due to their belief that it spread superstitions and that the Coptic practice of honoring saints and displaying their icons in the church was a pagan practice. The Coptic Church was in a sense perplexed. These Protestant missionaries were attempting to bring Christianity to Copts, but weren't Copts already Christians? The bishop of Asyut famously replied to a missionary who told him he attempted to bring Copts to live with Christ: "We have been living with Christ for more than eighteen hundred years, how long have you been living with him?"

Faced with the Protestant assault on the very foundation of Coptic Orthodoxy, especially in the south, Demetrius undertook a long trip there to visit his community, trying to stop the missionaries' success. His efforts were ultimately futile. Modernity had ushered in a new competition for the hearts and souls of Copts and in such an open market, the old Coptic Church had few weapons to compete. From a community that officially numbered six hundred in 1875, the Protestant community grew to twenty-nine thousand by 1904, surpassing the Catholic community for the first time.

The growth of the Protestant threat forced the Coptic Church to develop answers to new points of difference. While Coptic counter-Catholic literature is abundant from earlier historical periods, the first major work against Protestant teachings and in defense of Orthodox beliefs appears by the 1890s. The lectures of Habib Guirguis, whom we will meet later in history, were split between traditional counter-Catholic arguments dealing with Peter's primacy among the Apostles, papal infallibility, the nature of Christ, the rejection of Purgatory, Immaculate Conception, and priestly celibacy, and newer topics aimed at defending Coptic beliefs against Protestant criticisms such as salvation by faith, icons, sacraments, intercession of saints, monasticism, and fasting.

Demetrius's death in 1870 left the papal throne empty for four years. During those years, leaders of the Coptic laity managed to convince the locum tenens[4] to agree to the establishment of a Milli Council (Coptic Community Council) composed of leading members of the laity to help manage the church affairs. Using their influence with the government, they managed to secure a Khedival Decree in February 1874 setting the procedures for the selection of the council's members and their task. Having secured their role in managing the affairs of the church, they helped elect a new pope, Kyrillos V, later that year in November.

Kyrillos V was born in 1824; by the time he was elected pope in 1874, he was already an old man. He had spent his years as a monk busy copying ancient manuscripts. Some later historians claimed that before being selected he had given his endorsement to the

---

4. Upon the death of a pope and until the selection of his successor, the Holy Synod appoints one of its members, a bishop, as locum tenens. His job is to simply manage the daily affairs of the church until a new pope is elected.

establishment of the Milli Council. Whether the partisans of the council had secured his promise or simply assumed he could not challenge their plans is still a matter of debate. In any case, a simple monk, fifty years old, was hardly a threat to the Coptic beys who were well established in the government service. Nothing at his disposal was equal to their power. Or so they thought. To their utter bewilderment, the aging monk not only sat at the papal throne for fifty-three years until he died at the age of 103 in 1927, but managed to rout the great pashas and beys.

Who were those members of the Coptic elite that called for the establishment of the Milli Council and what did they aim to achieve? These men were largely the product of the schools established by Kyrillos IV. After receiving their education, they entered the service of the state and rose to prominence as civil servants. They were led by men such as Boutros Ghali Pasha. The cause to which they rallied was a bit more complicated than they were. Partly, the call for the members of a community to manage its affairs fits perfectly into the democratic spirit of the age. On the other hand, it was to a great extent a copy of similar actions and councils that had sprung up throughout the Ottoman Empire to administer the affairs of their communities. The Jewish community council was established in Egypt in 1854 and the Armenian council in 1864. Copts were thus acting within the framework of the Ottoman Millet System, though technically they were never one of the Millets.

These men were also quite influenced by the spread of Protestant ideas in Egypt. The Protestant teaching, with its emphasis on a personal message of salvation and a personal relationship with God and its downplaying of the role of high clergy, certainly helped stir the spirit of the laity making it more aware of its important role in the church. Another element in the mix was the social and economic divide between the clergy and the leading members of the laity. The clergy largely came from the lower classes of society. In the eyes of the newly educated and powerful state servants, these ignorant monks and priests were not well equipped to deal with administrative matters. They might be able to perform prayers, but they had no clue as how to manage the huge endowments of the church. It was they, the great civil servants, who were well equipped to deal with such matters. The church, while poor, had at its disposal huge endowments. If the council partisans could take over control of these, they could prevent their current misuse and better manage them to the benefit of the whole community.

What the council partisans never expected was that the man who had just become pope had an iron will, against which their attempts would prove ineffective. Kyrillos did not welcome their interference in what he naturally viewed as his domain. Why should he accept shackles imposed on his authority that none of his predecessors had had to suffer? By not attending the council meetings and refusing to give them access to the church's finances and endowments, he managed to curtail the council until it fizzled out. In May 1883, the council partisans renewed their efforts and managed to obtain a new Khedival Decree to hold elections. Like its predecessor, within a few months, the council came to naught.

Learning from their previous mistakes, the council supporters were determined not to fail for a third time. In July 1892 they managed to obtain another Khedival Decree to hold new elections. The right of the laity to participate in the management of the church became their rallying cry. Kyrillos V refused to allow them entry into the patriarchate to hold new elections, but, under the protection of the police and under the supervision of the Cairo governor, they held one anyway. Using their connections, they were in a better position than the pope to use government force for their benefit. Kyrillos tried to meet the khedive to present his case, but was humiliated when informed that the khedive had refused to grant him an audience. His appeal to the foreign counselors also failed. The counselors, as modern men, naturally sympathized with the partisans of reform and self-government. The same sympathy was shared by the British agent in Egypt, Lord Cromer, who for all practical purposes was the real ruler of the country.

After some failed mediation efforts, and utterly convinced that there was no possibility of working alongside Kyrillos, the laity managed to find a supporter for their efforts among the clergy, in the person of Bishop Athanasius of Sanabu, whom they convinced to travel to Cairo. They secured government approval of his appointment as vicar general replacing Kyrillos as chairman of the council and hence relieving him of his administrative duties. In Athanasius, they thought they had secured an ally and handed Kyrillos a clear defeat. What they did not anticipate was the pope's reaction. He ordered his bishops to await the travelling bishop at the train station and inform him that if he entered Cairo he would be excommunicated. Undeterred, Athanasius continued his journey and upon attempting entry into the patriarchate found its doors shut in his face. The council supporters had had enough with Kyrillos V. Again using their government connections, they obtained the government's approval of the appointment of the Sanabu bishop as locum tenens deposing Kyrillos and on September 1, 1892, received an order for the pope's banishment to a monastery in the desert. Surrounded by the police, the pope submitted and, accompanied by the police, travelled to the desert. His opponents' triumph was now complete.

What the pashas and beys had not considered in their calculations was the spiritual power the pope possessed. They had at their disposal the full power of the state, but he had something much more powerful: his clout as pope. Copts were horrified at his treatment. If some of them sympathized with the council's demands, they were appalled by its actions. Churches were immediately abandoned. No Copt would pray in a church where the priest or bishop performing the service was a partisan of the council and thus had been excommunicated. Copts in Cairo either crossed the Nile to Giza, whose bishop supported his Holy Father or prayed at the Armenian church. The bishop of Sanabu himself, while still supporting the council, did not dare present himself for communion. Even he was fully aware of the authority of the pope and did not question his excommunication. Bishops abandoned their dioceses and went to the monasteries. Priests loyal to the pope, who were the absolute majority, stopped performing services. There were no more marriage services, newborns were not given baptism, and the dead did not receive their rites. The life of Copts, as Copts, had simply come to a halt.

The council and its supporters were at a complete loss as to what to do. They tried inviting the bishops to a Holy Synod meeting to find a way out. The few bishops who attended demanded the return of the pope and refused to revoke the excommunications declaring that only Kyrillos V could remove them. Completely defeated, they were forced to ask the government for the return of Kyrillos. The new khedive, Abbas Helmi, and his new prime minister, Riad Pasha, were more favorably disposed towards the pope. The bishop of Sanabu resigned on January 14, 1893, and six days later, on January 20, the order for the pope's return was issued. He entered Cairo a few days later. Thousands of people gathered to greet him and accompany his triumphant march into the city; the women threw flowers at his cart and the men removed its horses and pulled the cart themselves, in ultimate testimony to his complete triumph.

The lines in the battle between clergy and laity had been drawn. The new Coptic elite had played its best hand and had failed miserably. While the Milli Council would be reestablished under

Kyrillos in 1906 and under his successors, the council partisans would never be able to muster the will or the ability to challenge the men sitting on the papal throne in the way they did in 1892. For perhaps the first time since the Council of Chalcedon, the earthly powers had attempted to challenge the successor of St. Mark on the seat of Alexandria. Like his predecessors Athanasius and Dioscorous, Kyrillos could rely on his religious power as pope and, more importantly, on the active support of his people.

One development however could not be ignored. The new Coptic elite had used its influence in the state to its advantage. The pope had been humiliated initially and then forced into exile. Involving the government in internal church affairs had been a useful tool in the hands of the partisans of the council, but the lesson of the power such an intervention entailed would not be lost on the clergy. In 1912, Kyrillos managed to convince the government to change the laws of the council in his favor to grant him more powers. In 1927, with the pope near death, the pendulum swung in the other direction and it was the council partisans who were able to use their influence with the government and pass a new law in their favor. Successors of Kyrillos V would find it beneficial to use the government's power in their favor further consolidating their power over the church. On the other hand, Kyrillos's triumph over the laity made the government well aware of where the real power over Copts lay. Successive governments would attempt to control or work together with the clergy in order to control Copts. Similarly, the eyes of the council members were opened to the immense powers at the disposal of the pope; they would attempt to affect and control future papal elections in order to put someone favorable to their views on the papal throne. The episode of 1892 would have profound implications for the future of the church, and Copts in general.

Kyrillos V sat on the papal throne for fifty-four years. During his long reign he focused his efforts on reviving the church. He travelled to the south of Egypt in 1904 and again in 1908 to counter Protestant missionaries. Twenty-three Coptic schools were established between 1873 and 1878. By 1907 there were forty-six schools with 21,675 students. By 1910, the number of students had reached 28,962. Copts were being educated at a faster rate than their Muslim counterparts. The pope urged Copts to transfer their sons and daughters from the missionaries' schools to the new Coptic ones. He urged the government to teach Christianity to Christian students in government schools just as their Muslim counterparts were being taught Islam. Furthermore, in 1903 he opened special technical schools for carpenters and housekeeping schools for women. On November 29, 1893, and for the first time in probably more than fourteen hundred years, a school of theology was established in Egypt. The Coptic Theological Seminary was the successor of the great Catechetical School of Alexandria. Kyrillos V further established three schools dedicated to the education of monks. He sent students to the Theological School in Athens to learn theology. He sponsored the efforts of Ekladious Labib to bring the Coptic language to life again thereby saving it from extinction.

The life of Kyrillos V and his efforts to revive the Coptic Church were tied to his deacon and disciple, Habib Guirguis (1876–1951). Habib, who was educated in the Coptic school, became the standard bearer of Orthodoxy in Egypt and its greatest champion. As one of the first students in the new Coptic Theological Seminary, he soon showed his brilliance and became his classmates' teacher. In 1918, he became dean of the seminary. He was well aware of the weakness of the Orthodox teaching and the threat the missionaries posed. To that end, he never married and dedicated his life to the revival of the Coptic Church. A prolific writer, he published more than thirty books as well as a magazine, *El Karma*, to spread Orthodox beliefs among Copts. Education was his focus. He taught, published, preached, and mentored generations of Copts. In the first years of the century he laid the cornerstone of what would become the Sunday School Movement by gathering the government school's Coptic students and teaching them the tenets of their faith. This small step gave rise to the General Committee of Sunday Schools in 1918. These schools were instrumental in creating the Coptic revival which soon spread throughout the country. The Coptic revival of the 1950s and the leaders of the Coptic Church since can all be traced to the initiatives he undertook.

The efforts taken by Kyrillos IV to reform the Coptic Church and educate Copts had now split into two separate paths that could not be reconciled. On one fork were the new Coptic elite, influenced by the spirit of the age and the Protestant missionaries with their reforming projects. On the other, the old clergy led by the pope attempted to defend their terrain. Soon enough a third path would emerge. The seeds that Habib Guirguis had planted would grow into a movement that would attempt to revive Coptic Orthodoxy to counter the influence of the missionaries and stop their encroachment on what they viewed as theirs: Copts. Reform inspired by the Protestant missionaries and setting them as a model for a more modern church and community vs. revival as a reaction and counter to the Protestant missionaries became the identities of the two roads.

CHAPTER FIVE

We the . . . ?
Forming a National Identity

THE LORD AND HIS BOYS

THE EGYPT OF 1879 WAS NEAR BOILING POINT. Ismail's extravagant spending had not only brought about his downfall, but had also permitted foreign intervention in Egyptian affairs to protect the rights of lenders. Desperate, Ismail had attempted to foster anti-foreign sentiments in order to counter foreign interference, but his efforts were unsuccessful in saving him from his eventual demise. At the same time, a new elite was rising whose interests and education naturally drove a concern for public affairs. His son, Tawfik, was to reap the consequences of these phenomena.

The brief three-year period between 1879 and 1882 witnessed the escalation of the conflict along three interlinked axes; anti-foreign agitation, anti-Turkish agitation, and civil vs. military competition. Orabi Pasha, the military officer who emerged as the key figure in these years, managed to eclipse the civilians and ensure a military domination of the national struggle. What started as a limited military insurrection by Egyptian officers against Turkish officers' domination of the military soon became a nationalist struggle against both Khedive Tawfik and the interference of European powers. That nationalist struggle was inherently contradictory given its internal anti-Turkish agitation while framing its cause as pro-Ottoman against European powers. Orabi's brief moment of domination was soon crushed by a British invasion.

The British invasion began as a short-term intervention with the goal of ending the insurrection, restoring the authority of the khedive, protecting the European minorities in Egypt, stabilizing the country, and thus guaranteeing its adherence to its financial obligations. Soon enough, any illusion of the short-term nature of the occupation was dispelled by reality. Once they were in Egypt, the British could not leave even if they wanted to. There was simply too much at stake given their investment in the Suez Canal, and with it the route to India, and their need to "guide Egyptians" to be able to manage the country's affairs. At the head of the British occupation stood one man, Evelyn Baring (Lord Cromer), upon whose shoulders fell the task of governing Egypt.

Mohamed Ali is often credited as the founder of modern Egypt. Such a portrayal wrongly diminishes the role Cromer played in lifting the country up from its dysfunctional state and shaping it into its modern form. The Lord, as Egyptians came to know him, was the effective ruler of the country from 1883 until 1907. He was guided throughout his rule of Egypt by two contradictory principles: liberalism and imperialism.

First was his belief, as a liberal of his times, in limited government. The less the government interfered in the country's economy and the lives of its citizens the better. He felt compassion for the *fellah* (peasant) and sought to "liberate" him from government tyranny. Secondly, as a result of his experience in India, he did not favor local rule and autonomy. This was based on his firm belief in a clear divide between East and West and that it was only with the guiding hand of the West that the East could advance. This belief in the clear divide between the two worlds made him quite skeptical regarding the ability of Easterners to overcome the deficiencies in their culture[1] and become similar to Westerners. His policies were thus framed as benevolent British rule through hundreds of advisors and administrators in Egyptian ministries who aimed at helping the peasants, combined with a clear mistrust of the local elite, who were attempting to imitate the West.

Lord Cromer's first task was to solve the country's financial mess. Through effective governance and administrative measures he largely succeeded in that mission. Simultaneously, though at first reluctantly, he undertook massive hydraulics and irrigation projects aimed at developing the country's agricultural capabilities. His lack of faith in local governance led him to view the governorship of Egypt as merely an administrative task, which was detached from any political dimensions. The area, to which he devoted the least attention, if any at all, was education. Lord Cromer was quite aware that an increase in educated Egyptians greater than the capacity of the civil service to absorb it would be quite dangerous to the country's stability. He severely decreased government spending on education with the aim of producing only the necessary bureaucrats. In 1882 there were twenty-eight government primary schools and two secondary schools in Egypt. By 1907, there were thirty-two primary and four secondary schools. The secondary schools were producing one hundred graduates a year in a population of eleven million. Between 1882 and 1917, the illiteracy rate remained at 91 percent among men, with the rate among women at 99.7 percent.

---

1. For Lord Cromer, all Eastern cultures were the same. India was not different from Egypt.

While Lord Cromer was able to control governmental education, his hands were tied, by the capitulations,* to interfere in private European education and missionary schools which expanded
enormously during those years. Students were increasingly sent by
their parents to Europe, especially France, to study. Egyptians
sought government jobs because they were the route to economic
security as well as the possibility of moving up the social ladder.
Modern education was the entry gate to that future. Despite
Cromer's efforts, a massive civil service was being created.

Khedive Abbas Helmi's ascension to the throne in 1892 ushered
in a period of conflict with Lord Cromer. Unlike his father, Tawfik,
Abbas Helmi harbored dreams of ruling Egypt in practice and not
just in name. He gathered around him members of the new emerging Egyptian elite and attempted to fan anti-British sentiments
among them. Abbas's efforts would eventually lead to the division
of the emerging nationalist movement into pro-khedive and pro-
British camps with considerable maneuvering room between the two.

The first group, which would later become the National Party,
was led by the young firebrand Mustafa Kamil (1874–1908).
Supporting the new khedive's efforts to curb the power of the
British, he framed his nationalist fever for Egypt as a nation.
Mustafa Kamil's "Egypt," however, was an unidentified nation. A
romantic nationalist, he preached the love of Egypt paying little
attention to the contradictions between his pan-Islamic, pro-
sultan, and initially pro-khedive rhetoric and Egyptian nationalism. That contradiction became most apparent during the 1906
Aqaba incident. Faced with a struggle between the British occupier and the Ottoman Sultan as to Egypt's exact eastern borders,

---

* Grants issued by the Ottoman Sultans to European powers giving their
citizens who reside or trade with the Ottoman Empire certain privileges and
rights.

he supported the sultan's rights at the expense of Egyptian territorial rights.

That incident highlighted the break between those such as Mustafa Kamil who still harbored pan-Islamic dreams on the one hand, and Ahmed Lutfi El Sayed (1872–1963) and his colleagues who sought to define the new Egyptian nation in territorial terms on the other. Unlike Kamil, Lutfi El Sayed completely rejected any form of nationalism that sought to place Egypt in a larger entity than its borders, be it pan-Islamic, pro-Ottoman or Arab Nationalist. For him, Egypt had a distinct core reaching back to the pharaohs. While influenced by various currents throughout the centuries, that core had remained intact and developed a distinct Egyptian personality. While originally a friend of the Muslim reformer Mohamed Abduh (1849–1905), Lutfi El Sayed disagreed with Abduh on the latter's argument for a return to the Salaf[2] as a model. The Salaf were the very reason for decline and Lutfi El Sayed argued that Egypt needed to abandon them and adopt change. Egypt needed to build its modernization on the Greek and Roman classics just as Europe had done.

Underlying Lutfi El Sayed's writings was an esoteric argument that he dared not make clear concerning the matter of Islam. While Abduh sought to find ways to bridge the gap between Islam and modernity by arguing that Islam was a secular religion in the sense of having no clergy and was inherently the religion of reason and science, Lutfi El Sayed understood them as contradictory. His personal religious views notwithstanding, he explicitly wanted to banish Islam from the public sphere. Like Lord Cromer,

---

2. The term "Salaf" is literarily translated as predecessors. It is a loose term that describes Muslims who lived during the three first centuries of Islam. The term "Devout Salaf" refers to the companions of the Prophet Mohamed and the two generations who followed them and received the true essence of the faith.

he believed that Islam was an obstacle to modernization and that attempts to reform or undermine it would result in the problem exploding and destroying the modernization project. Islam was a landmine better left untouched. Unlike Lord Cromer, however, he was a firm believer in human progress. Influenced by Darwinism and its social manifestations, he believed that eventually the problem would simply disappear over time. Egyptians would grow more secular and progressive, and religion would be limited to the private sphere. Lutfi El Sayed and his friends were weaned on the French Enlightenment and believed in its promises. This understanding would have profound implications for the emerging Egyptian nationalism that he helped shape, its views of Islam, and most important for this book, its views of Copts.

The new elite were made up of an administrative bourgeoisie with strong rural ties. The emergence of an industrial and mercantile bourgeoisie would have to wait until after the First World War. Modernization was being introduced in accelerating speed. The printing press was producing translations of European works, from French mostly,[3] to an eager growing audience. Shibli Shumayil (1860–1916) and Farah Antun (1874–1922), were two Syrian immigrants residing in Egypt who helped introduce European ideas to the Egyptian public through their writings. Darwin's theory of evolution had a huge impact on their minds. The number of newspapers was increasing and the increase in the number of lawyers and teachers widened their audience. The class of disconnected intellectuals that Lord Cromer feared most had emerged under his very nose and despite his best efforts.

Lutfi El Sayed and his friends first established their newspaper, *Al Jarida,* in July 1907. On the September 20, 1907, as a result of

---

3. The only clear Anglophone in the new emerging intellectuals of the time was Ahmed Fathy Zaghloul, Saad's brother, who died a young man.

the Aqaba incident and the widening gap between them and Mustafa Kamil, they formed the Umma (Nation) Party. The Umma Party was made up of members of the new emerging Egyptian elite. They viewed the khedive, and the old Turkish elite as their main competitors. They had risen in the service of the British and feared a more powerful khedive as the main threat to the nation's interests. They were thus willing to accommodate the British occupation as long as it meant their chance to destroy the old elite.

The new elite had been friends of Mohamed Abduh, but had grown disillusioned at the prospects of reforming Islam that he advocated. The struggle for independence and greater autonomy was a concern for them, but prerequisites to independence were required. Egypt was no less a nation than Bulgaria or Serbia, but it needed to convince the world that it was a civilized nation, one that possessed a great past and the prospect of building a future.[4] Education was the route to gaining those prerequisites. It was this circle of intellectuals who championed the cause of establishing the Egyptian University, which they finally did in December 1908. By abandoning any serious attempt to reform Al Azhar, they had cemented the dual nature of the Egyptian educational system which divided in two separate routes. Kassem Amin, a member of this circle, championed women's rights. A nation could not stand on its feet with half of its people jailed behind a wall of ignorance and tradition. For them, Mustafa Kamil and his approach were wrong. Negotiating with the British for more local autonomy was a political task, to be conducted by this new elite and that did not involve the masses. They did not resort to the inflammatory and

---

4. Egyptian nationalist writings at the time are abundant with comparisons to the new nations emerging in Eastern Europe. Egypt had begun its modernization before them, and surely if they could gain their independence, so could Egypt.

demagogic rhetoric of Kamil. Egypt, they reasoned, should not attempt to run before it had first learned how to walk.

Defining Egypt

The main competitors to the new elite were the old Turkish elite and Syrian immigrants who were increasingly employed by the British. In 1892, a decree was issued limiting government employment to Egyptians. Egyptians were defined as either those born in the country or Ottoman subjects residing in the country for the past fifteen years. More limiting decrees would be issued in the future and would indicate the growing ability of the new elite to push aside its competitors. The numerous British civil servants spread in Egyptian ministries were another obstacle to the advancement of the new elite and anger towards the British, especially given their arrogance towards Egyptians, played a key role in kindling the fires of resentment towards the occupation.

The new circle of intellectuals had come a long way from their days as friends and disciples of Mohamed Abduh. They had completely abandoned Islam as the basis for politics and the nation and wanted to limit religion to the private sphere. They replaced Islam with nationalism on territorial basis. The Egyptian nation, as Lutfi El Sayed and his colleagues argued, had kept a pharaonic core throughout the centuries. The new Egypt they conceived was not new at all. They traced it to the ancient past. While the long years of Islamic Egypt had made the pharaohs little more than an ancient unfamiliar heritage, the European obsession with the pharaohs had managed to impress Egyptian minds. If the world stood in awe of that great ancient civilization, it was but natural that the Sons of the Nile take pride in their heritage and attempt to claim it for their national project. Later on, the discovery of the tomb of

Tutankhamen would lead to a huge fascination with the pharaonic past and would leave an impact on contemporary Egyptian art as evidenced by Saad Zaghloul's tomb.

While political nationalism is certainly a modern phenomenon born out of modernity, for the nationalist ideologue, the nation always existed. This led to absurd attempts to paint Egyptian history as an unbroken chain of nationalist struggle against occupiers. Arguments for the purity of pharaonic blood were accompanied by the proliferation of articles tracing the nationalist struggle of the pharaohs against the Hyksos, c. 1800 BC, and against every new occupier from the Persians, the Ptolemaic, and the Romans. Historical figures such as Ahmose, were imagined and discovered as nationalist heroes as is evidenced by Naguib Mahfouz's early novels.[5]

It was from this foundation that the National Unity discourse finally emerged and it is precisely for this reason that the Coptic question was problematic. Egypt was one homogeneous nation. Diversity was neither acknowledged nor tolerated. In a sense, nationalism was understood as a hat. One could not wear more than one. Either one was an Egyptian or something else, but not both.[6] This meant that any suggestion by Copts that they formed a distinct nation was not only not welcomed but had to be suppressed. Copts and Muslims were described as two elements of the Egyptian nation. They had lived in perfect harmony for centuries. If there were any tensions between them today it was only due to Western attempts to divide and rule. The Egyptian nation had been

---

5. During the late '30s and early '40s Naguib Mahfouz wrote: *Old Egypt* (1932), *Mockery of the Fates* (1939), *Rhadopis of Nubia* (1943), and *The Struggle of Thebes* (1944), all of which dealt with pharaonic history.

6. I owe the analogy to Linda Colley who wrote in her book *Britons: Forging the Nation 1707–1837* that "identities are not like hats. Human beings can and do put on several at a time."

in eternal struggle against occupiers. The church division after the Council of Chalcedon was thus described in nationalist terms; Copts had risen against Byzantine hegemony.[7] Copts had welcomed the Muslims whom they saw as liberators, and had been in constant unity since as exemplified by the Crusades. It was the missionaries and the occupiers who tried to divide them.

The most striking aspect of the National Unity discourse as adopted by the early intellectuals, and as it continues to be propagated today, is its inherent contradiction between claiming Egypt as a homogeneous nation and highlighting the unity between two distinct and separate elements. This discourse framed Copts as not only a distinct group but more importantly as a group in the first place. In this sense, while it was demanded that the Copt escape his Coptness in order to be a member of the Egyptian nation, he could not escape it. No matter what he did, he was viewed and understood as a Copt.

Besides its inherent contradiction, the Egyptian nationalist discourse as framed by Lutfi El Sayed and his colleagues was problematic for Copts for two reasons. First, it did not tolerate Coptic claims of exclusive possession of the pharaonic past. If Copts claimed they were the true descendents of the pharaohs that would undermine the very basis of Egyptian nationalism. Secondly, any Coptic grievances had to be suppressed. Discrimination against Copts did not fit the nationalist narrative. The mythology of the eternal unity had to be maintained. It is within this context that the Umma Party's reaction in the future to the Coptic Conference should be understood.

---

7. Curiously, this approach has not been limited to Egyptian nationalist intellectuals but has found new appeal among Western scholars who see an imperialist hegemony at every corner of history, modern or pre-modern. Absurd descriptions of colonialism and anti-colonialism are abundant in the currently dominant Middle East studies school.

This is not to say that Lutfi El Sayed and his colleagues were fanatics. They were not anti-Christian as much as they were anti-Coptic. They were men guided by their belief in the Enlightenment, evolutionary progress, and the nationalist ideas of Europe. Underlying their views was the problem of Islam. Unlike their old friend Abduh, and like their mentor Cromer, they believed that Islam and modernity were contradictory. They anticipated that this contradiction would be solved by time as a result of human progress. If they were against any discussion of the Coptic problem, it was not because they were inherently predisposed against Copts. It was because they feared that such discussion would open the door to the problem they feared the most: to the time bomb waiting for explosion, to Islam.

Copts under British Rule

The fact that Egypt was occupied by a "Christian nation" posed problems not only for the Muslim majority but also for Copts. Certainly, some Copts welcomed the arrival of British troops both out of fear of the upheaval Orabi had unleashed and because they expected more favorable treatment at the hands of the British. Soon enough, these hopes faded away. Unlike the French in the Levant who favored the religious and ethnic minorities there, the British in Egypt did not favor Copts. In fact, a reverse favoritism towards the Muslim majority was maintained. In 1889, Lord Cromer made his views on the matter known to his superiors in Britain, writing that he took it for granted that it was better to govern through Muslims rather than Christians. The reasons behind such a position deserve consideration.

First was the matter of how Copts were viewed by the British occupation. While some Europeans felt an attraction to the ancient church, many, and certainly Lord Cromer, viewed Copts unfavorably. They did not possess the Christian virtues, he reasoned. Long centuries of coexistence with and subjection to Muslims had made them indistinguishable from Muslims in their habits. Copts were accused of being deceitful and cowards in their submission to authority. Secondly, Egypt's ethnic and religious composition was different from that of the Levant with its mosaic of minorities. A policy favoring Muslims would ensure the country's tranquility. Cromer viewed Muslims as fanatics and had little faith in their tolerance should the British appoint Copts to higher positions. Thirdly, while some Copts were favorable to the British occupation, most, out of fear or genuine dislike, were not. There was no reason to grant them any privileges.

This policy was manifested in appointments to high-ranking government positions. While under Mohamed Ali, Copts had been appointed as district governors, and Said had appointed an Armenian Christian as governor of Sudan, the British reserved that position for Muslims, arguing that the nature of the governor's job necessitated him being Muslim given the need for the local population to respect his authority. In the civil service, a lot of jobs historically occupied by Copts were given to Syrian immigrants. The Syrian immigration to Egypt had accelerated after the 1860 disturbances in Lebanon. For the British, the Syrians were ideal candidates to fill government jobs. They were better educated than Egyptians, Muslims, and Christian alike, as well as more modern and more similar to Europeans.

For Copts this posed a dilemma. Their traditional roles were being taken over by Syrians and by newly educated Muslims, while their paths to the new jobs opening in the government services were blocked. There seemed to be an invisible ceiling they could not pass. Modernization had undermined their traditional roles but had not replaced them with new opportunities.

This is not to suggest that Copts did not gain more equality in all areas during the years of the British occupation. Schools that had been traditionally closed to Copts were finally opened to them during that period. Copts entered the School of Engineering for the first time in 1899, the School of Medicine in 1886, the School of Law in 1887, the Teachers School in 1889, and the Endowments School in 1889. These new education venues gave Copts access to new jobs, especially in the private sector. However, these developments were not the result of British efforts but rather the natural development of the steps taken earlier by Ismail.

Boutros Ghali was the leading Coptic civil servant during those years. He had played an important role in internal Coptic affairs leading the Milli Council in its battle with Kyrillos V over the religious endowments, as well as mediating between the more militant elements in the council and the pope. He had risen in government service, became the first Copt to be awarded the title of pasha in 1882, appointed finance minister in 1893, and then foreign minister. During his long career he had won the trust of both Lord Cromer and Khedive Abbas Helmi, a seemingly impossible task. His government service had made him party to a number of controversial decisions that angered the nationalist movement in Egypt.

The new British Consul-General in Egypt, Sir Eldon Gorst, who replaced Cromer in 1907, adopted a different policy from Cromer in terms of his relationship with the khedive. He preferred cooperation to confrontation and the new government in London was in favor of more local autonomy. As a result, while initially preferring another candidate for the job of prime minister, he concurred with Abbas Helmi's advocacy for Ghali. Gorst had indicated that Boutros Ghali was qualified for the job, but that his religion removed him from consideration. The khedive, whether out of a desire to prove that the question of religion was irrelevant or preferring Ghali to the other candidate as more adaptable to his views, argued that Ghali should be appointed.

Boutros Ghali served as prime minister from November 12, 1908, until his assassination on February 20, 1910. He was the first Coptic prime minister though not the first Christian as Nubar had occupied that post earlier. But while Nubar's appointment was not entirely welcomed, Ghali's was seen as a serious affront to Muslims. A foreign Christian was one thing, a local one was another. The leading Egyptian intellectual, Abbas Mahmoud El Akkad, wrote at the time that the appointment was insulting to Muslim honor as it suggested no qualified Muslim existed. Mustafa Kamil's newspaper framed its opposition to the appointment as only on political grounds rather than religious ones.

Ghali was assassinated by a young nationalist, Ibrahim El Wardani, in 1910. While the assassin's motives were political, the killing was celebrated in the street as a religious one. "El Wardani killed El Nossrani"[8] was the chant of the Cairo mob. El Wardani's lawyer was none other than Ahmed Lutfi El Sayed. Egypt's mufti refused to endorse the death penalty passed on El Wardani, though the sentence was carried out anyway. Another Christian was appointed in the cabinet to maintain Christian representation, but by appointing a Catholic of Syrian origins, the British were practically adding insult to injury as far as the Copts were concerned. What made the matter worse was that communal relations between Copts and Muslims were at a critical juncture with a fully fledged press war taking place between them.

The war had started in June 1908 with an article critical of Islamic history appearing in *El Watan,* a leading Coptic newspaper.

---

8. The word Nossrani comes from Nassara, the term the Quran and hence Islamists use instead of Christians. Its origins lie either in the Arabic word "ansar" (supporters) to describe those who followed Christ or the city of Nazareth.

The very next day, Sheikh Abdel Aziz Gawish began a series of articles in *Al Liwa*, the official National Party newspaper, under the title "Islam alien in its own land." Other Muslim owned newspapers joined the fray with Abbas El Akkad, a leading figure in the anti-Coptic tirade. Lutfi El Sayed's *Al Jarida*, while not joining the attacks, refrained from publishing articles written by Copts attacking Gawish, which led Coptic newspapers to remark that on the Coptic issue, there was no difference between Lutfi El Sayed and Sheikh Gawish. Copts noted that while the British authorities penalized the Coptic newspapers, no such action was taken against the Muslim ones. Anything written however by the others paled next to what Gawish wrote. A section of one of the articles is worth quoting in full:

> Copts should be kicked to death. They still have faces and bodies similar to those of demons and monkeys, which is proof that they hide poisonous spirits within their evil soul. The fact that they exist in the world confirms Darwin's theory that human beings are generated from monkeys: You sons of adulterous women, have you become so foolhardy that you should start and abuse the Muslim faith. The curse of Allah on You! . . . . You tails of camels, with your monkey faces! You bones of bodies! You poor dreaming fools! You sons of mean rogues! Is it with such acts that people should win renown?[9]

THE TWO CONFERENCES

A call for a Coptic Conference had emerged before the assassination of Boutros Ghali with the initial date for its convocation

---

9. The quote appears in Robert Tignor's *Modernization and British Colonial Rule in Egypt, 1882–1914.*

February 24, 1910. Ghali's assassination four days earlier not
only moved the date a year later, but also impacted the very reason for the conference. The idea of the conference had originated
from the group of reformers inside the Coptic Church Milli
Council as well as those who had converted to Protestantism.
With the collapse of the previous Milli Council in 1909, those
reformers were looking for ways to pressure the church hierarchy.[10] The assassination of Ghali altered the direction of the conference and turned it into a forum to discuss Coptic grievances.

The conference convened on the March 6, 1911 in Asyut, the
natural choice given that the leaders of the conference all came
from Upper Egypt with few Cairenes participating. Even until
1917, 76 percent of Orthodox Copts lived in Upper Egypt with
Asyut as the capital of the Christian presence. Moreover, it had
become the center of Protestant missionaries among Copts which
resulted in the conversion of leading families in the city. Protestants were disproportionately represented in Upper Egypt with
91 percent of them living there. Thirdly, Asyut had a pro-reform
patron in the person of Bishop Macarius, of whom we will hear a
great deal later.

In total 1,150 Copts gathered for the conference, an impressive
number by the standards of the time. To become a delegate, each
had been required to gather the signatures of at least ten Copts to
affirm the representative nature of the conference. The conference
agreed to five demands which they hoped to present to the khedive
and implicitly to the British occupation. The five demands were:

1. Copts working in the government should be allowed to take
   Sunday off so as not to be forced to work on the Sabbath.

---

10. I owe this insight to Mourad Takawi's outstanding unpublished thesis
"Modernizing the Coptic Community: The Laity-Clergy Struggle for Communal Representation and the Road to the 1911 Asyut Congress."

2. Appointments and promotions in government jobs should be based on qualifications and capabilities. Copts should have an equal chance and not be denied these posts.
3. An electoral system that allows minority representation should be devised. The Belgian model was suggested.
4. Copts should be able to have equal access to education. In light of government spending on schools solely devoted to Muslims, taxes levied for the purpose of education should not be paid by Copts. Alternatively the government should fund Christian schools.
5. Government funding for charities should be given equally to Christian and Muslim organization regardless of their religion.

The Copts of 1911 were in a precarious position. They were fearful of the pan-Islamist slogans that had dominated the nationalist struggle under Mustafa Kamil. His party had attracted few Copts such as Wissa Wassef and Sinot Hanna, who would play significant roles in the future with the Wafd Party and while the slogan "Egypt for the Egyptians" that the Umma Party raised was certainly appealing, the underlying themes of the party guaranteed that few Copts, if any, joined. Ghali's assassination and the religious undertone of the attacks on his legacy had brought those fears to the open. But if the nationalist movement had not been able to absorb the Copts, neither were the British. Copts had lost their traditional roles, and were not allowed to seek modern ones where they would be equal to Muslims. Modernity had removed many of the old chains on Coptic advancement, but new ones had appeared. These Copts were more urban and modern than their Muslim counterparts. Kyrillos IV efforts at education had borne their fruits and Copts were more likely to send their children to missionary schools.

The discovery of the glorious pharaonic past had given them an identity. They were the true descendents of the pharaohs, they argued. They had not been tainted by the Bedouin waves. They had kept their purity and were the original inhabitants of the country. True, many had converted, but those were the poorer they reasoned, those who could not buy their religious freedom by paying the *jizya*. The Copts viewed themselves as better and wealthier than their countrymen. Their ancient church had stood as a rock in front of wave after wave of persecution. It had not bent. It had not been broken. Forever persecuted, but never destroyed.

Reading the demands of 1911 today, one cannot escape a feeling of amusement and sorrow considering how advanced they were. Today, Copts would not dream of making such demands and are instead desperately seeking more basic needs. It is important to recognize this decrease in the level of demand especially when one compares it to the Muslim response, both to the conference and today.

The responses to the Coptic Conference varied. The Coptic Church did not look favorably at it, with the pope publicly stating his objection. While some attribute this stand to government pressure, the pope needed no encouragement to realize that the leaders of the conference were the same council diehards he had been fighting for so long. Bishop Macarius of Asyut welcomed the conference and opened its sessions with a speech, but he was already known as a champion of reform. The British shared the church's position although for different reasons. The conference was threatening the country's tranquility and thus posed a challenge to the equilibrium the British had maintained. Especially unwelcome was the attempt by Copts to speak directly to members of the British Parliament and attempts to bring Coptic grievances to their attention. Gorst was not receptive to any Coptic demands and ridiculed them both in letters to his superiors in

Britain and in his public statements. Most surprising was the position of the National Party which did not lead the incitement against the conference and, viewing it as a British attempt to divide the nation, chose largely to ignore it. The rest of the press attacked the conference describing it as a religious conspiracy.

The anti-Coptic banner was thus completely left for Lutfi El Sayed and his colleagues to flock to. As the conference was finishing its sessions, a call emerged for a Muslim Conference to be held. The Umma Party group immediately seized the opportunity, and encouraged by Gorst, managed to convince a former prime minister, Riad Pasha, to chair what they now called the Egyptian Conference. While they changed their conference's name to Egyptian instead of Muslim, its nature was indeed a Muslim response to Coptic demands, which makes the nationalist's claim all the more extraordinary, if not completely understandable.

The Egyptian Conference was held on April 29, 1911, and while including a speaker here and there from the National Party or the Reform Party, it was completely organized and dominated by the Umma Party. Participants included Mahmoud Soliman, Ali Shaarawi, Abdel Aziz Fahmy, Ahmed Lutfi El Sayed, and Mahmoud Aboul Nasr, all of whom were leaders of the Umma Party. The conference was thus the response not of the pan-Islamist branch of the Egyptian nationalist movement but of the Westernized, secular, liberal nationalists. This is worth remembering in light of the arguments they advocated in their conference and how indistinguishable they are from those adopted by Islamists today.

The conference opened with Riad Pasha's speech which declared that there was never a Coptic issue in the past and there should be no Coptic issue in the future. He argued that the country's conditions did not allow such a discussion to take place. He was followed by the reading of the Conference Report by Ahmed Lutfi El Sayed and Abdel Aziz Fahmy, which was most likely written by the former. It declared that "behind the Coptic Conference were hidden motives and organized conspiracies to harm the majority and to hurt national unity so that the nation becomes prey to foreign designs." The main themes of the long report were that Copts had secretly conspired in holding their conference, that by this action they had destroyed or harmed national unity, that they had attempted to use foreign powers to reach their aims, that they had attempted to portray Muslims as fanatics, that they claimed to constitute a separate nation, that their true aim was the subjection of the majority to their supremacy, and that they tried to obtain a special status. It refused to recognize the idea of the existence of a Coptic minority, and finally blamed foreign missionaries for creating the whole issue.

The report bluntly rejected the five demands of the Coptic Conference. Sunday could not become a holiday as such a suggestion was unpractical. Copts should not complain of not being appointed to certain positions, such discrimination was correct as certain positions, such as that of governor, required that a Muslim occupy them. Furthermore, Copts were already getting more than their fair share of jobs in government and in education. And they were showing favoritism to their co-religionists. On the other hand, a Muslim could not possibly show favoritism since he belonged to the majority. The Coptic Conference itself was proof that Copts favored their co-religionists. The report cited numbers to prove that Copts were over-represented in government ministries. It was not possible to teach Christianity in a *kuttab* where there were Muslim students. The report ended with an emphasis on the equality of all Egyptians and a call for Copts to refrain from actions harming national unity.

The long report was followed by more speeches, and while some focused on economic and social issues, the anti-Coptic theme continued to appear. One critic reasoned that the secret goal of the Coptic demand of making Sunday a holiday was to gradually change the government's religion. Another ridiculed Copts and portrayed them as a frightened minority. Those who had not converted to Islam had lived in isolation and thus developed the myths and fears associated with it. They had sought the help of the mighty British since they felt weak. They did not feel they were Egyptians. For some, the reason for the Coptic demands was the Muslims' leniency, the encouragement of the missionaries, and Copts' imagination that the British would support them. The government had been too lax with Copts by allowing them to keep their endowments and their own religious courts, and giving them three seats in the representative body. It was argued that Copts had not participated in Egypt's renaissance as none of them were sent in Mohamed Ali's student missions. It was demanded that only Islam be taught in government schools.

The conference's final report rejected all Coptic demands. It declared that Copts had exceeded all possible levels in the number of jobs they occupied and that the Egyptian government should investigate the excessive number of Copts and find a remedy to that problem.

While the Coptic demands of 1911 are far higher than anything Copts today would dream of, it is quite astonishing how the answers to Coptic demands have not changed at all. While these answers were originally written and championed by men who are described as liberals and seculars, today's advocates are mainly Islamists with a fair share of Arab nationalists. The themes championed at the Egyptian Conference of 1911 became the standard framework of dealing with the Coptic question. It is important to note how they have been developed today.

Riad's argument that there is no Coptic problem became the standard response for both the Egyptian government and many of the political elite. Whenever even small grievances are acknowledged, Riad's assertion that the country's situation can't allow holding such discussion is invoked.

Whenever Copts present their grievances, that very act is considered a threat to national unity. It is not the fact that there is a Coptic problem or that Copts are discriminated against that is threatening to national unity. Only when Copts complain is that sacred cow of national unity threatened. Any Coptic demands are declared sectarian in nature and thus inappropriate and indicative of Copts acting like a minority, which as every Egyptian politician from Lutfi El Sayed to President Mohamed Morsi would declare, they are not. The accusation of secret plans and organized conspiracies finds its modern echo in rumors of weapons stockpiled in monasteries and was taken to a whole new level by Sheikh El Ghazaly, a popular preacher who in the '70s authored a modern version of the Protocols of the Elders of Zion—only this time what might be called the Protocols of the Elders of Copts.

Coptic demands are seen as inherently unpatriotic as they seek to involve foreign powers in internal Egyptian affairs. Good patriotic Copts are thus expected to condemn reports by Western organizations on the lack of religious freedom in Egypt and to refrain from meeting their visiting delegations. Copts meeting with them are attempting to portray Muslims and Islam as fanatic. Furthermore, the emergence of Coptic demands is always the result of incitement or instigation by foreigners. These foreigners might be missionaries as they were at the time of the two conferences. Today, Israel has become the favorite scapegoat for Arab nationalists and Islamists whenever a sectarian incident occurs. Conspiracy theorists are no longer content with blaming Coptic demands on foreign powers, but have expanded the theory further blaming the attacks on Copts by Islamist groups on a secret Mossad plot to both harm national unity and tarnish the image of Islam and Egypt.

The liberal nationalists of 1911 saw the Coptic identity as a threat to their idea of the Egyptian nation. There could be no separate identity or nation within the borders of Egypt. President Sadat would take this argument further accusing Pope Shenouda III in 1981 of attempting to build a separate Coptic state in Asyut. Coptic demands for equality are today portrayed as they were in 1911 as an attempt to achieve a privileged position and subject Muslims to their supremacy. Attempting to change the Islamic face or core of Egypt became a favorite theme of Islamists. A ringing church bell, a tall church tower, a large church building, are all considered signs by hardliners that Christians have forgotten their appropriate place and aim to dominate Egypt. While the 1911 Egyptian Conference cited numbers of Copts in government service as proof that they were receiving more than their fair share and that they not Muslims were the fanatic party, today it is impossible to find any significant Coptic representation in government jobs to cite as an argument. Instead Islamists highlight Coptic success stories in business as proof of the community's domination. And while in 1911, an argument for certain positions, namely that of governor being allocated only to Muslims was advocated, each development in Egypt has excluded Copts from more and more positions.

Lutfi El Sayed's worst nightmare was close to materializing. The Coptic Conference had brought religion and the sectarian issue to the forefront of the national debate and that was not helpful to the dreams of the modernizers. Religious divide was becoming an obstacle to the progress they had in mind and, also importantly to them, Egypt's image abroad had suffered. How to convince the world that Egypt deserved autonomy, if it was viewed as barbaric and fanatic?

In 1911, Kitchener became the British Consul-General in Egypt. By 1913 he had succeeded in responding to one of the Coptic Conference's demands—that of representation—by enacting a new law for the newly elected chamber. It would hence be composed of sixty-six elected and seventeen appointed delegates. The seventeen who were appointed would include four Copts. Copts were put in the context of other minorities, real or imagined. Hence the system also included three seats for Bedouins as well as two merchants, one medical doctor, and one engineer. Whatever remained of the sectarian debate was soon eclipsed by the beginning of World War I.

CHAPTER SIX

The Rise and Fall of the Liberal Age

THE 1919 REVOLUTION

THE BRITISH SEVERED EGYPT'S FORMAL RELATIONSHIP with the Ottoman Empire upon the latter's entry in World War I. Distrustful of the loyalty of Khedive Abbas Helmi, they replaced him with his uncle, Hussein Kamel, as sultan and declared Egypt a British protectorate. Anger at the harsh economic conditions during World War I joined a long list of grievances Egyptians harbored towards the British occupation. Encouraged by President Wilson's Fourteen Points and the slogans of self-determination, Egypt's political class took the end of hostilities as an opportunity to push for a reexamination of Egypt's relationship with Britain and ultimately for independence. The idea of negotiating such an outcome was born within the ranks of the now inactive Umma Party.

Saad Zaghloul, an icon in the history of Egyptian nationalism, was not a newcomer to politics. He had been part of the circle that gathered around Muslim reformer Mohamed Abduh and, though not officially a member due to his government post as minister of education, he was closely associated with the Umma Party. He had married into the old Turkish aristocracy and had been a protégé of Lord Cromer. On November 13, 1918, together with Ali Shaarawi and Abdel Aziz Fahmi, two leaders of the Umma party, he requested an audience with the British high commissioner and demanded the formation of a delegation to attend the Peace Conference to negotiate Egyptian independence. When the high commissioner complained that they were not representative of the country, they began collecting signatures to form the Wafd (The Delegation) to represent the nation.

The news of their audience with the high commissioner reached the Coptic notables in their Coptic, Ramses Club. Coptic leaders were alarmed that the Wafd, which was composed of seven members, did not include a single Copt. Three Coptic leaders paid a visit to Zaghloul and inquired as to where he stood on that issue. Zaghloul assured them that Copts would be treated as equal Egyptian citizens and that he did not differentiate between Christians and Muslims. He further asked them to nominate a Copt to be part of the Wafd, which they did by naming Boutros Ghali's son, Wassef.

Future Egyptian historiography would depict the 1919 revolution as a moment of national unity that transcended sectarian issues. Christians and Muslims were both part of the national movement and overcame their differences. After a perceived low point in the relationship between the elements of the nation, they returned to their natural and historical unity. While 1919 did indeed represent a high point in sectarian relations, this was not the result of natural and eternal harmony but of concerted efforts by the man who led the nationalist struggle, Saad Zaghloul.

Unlike the other members of the Umma Party, Zaghloul had not taken part in the anti-Coptic activities of the preceding decade. That was both a result of his ministerial post and his personal inclinations. When Boutros Ghali was chosen as prime minister, Zaghloul wrote in his diary that he feared the press would make an issue out of a Copt being appointed and thus give credence to accusations of Egyptians being fanatics. As minister of education, in 1907 he introduced the teaching of Christianity to Christian students in government schools for the first time. As a result, Copts viewed him favorably. Throughout his later career, Zaghloul would stress the unity between Copts and Muslims both as a result of his personal views and out of a clear awareness that problems between the two communities would result in foreign accusations and thus hinder Egypt's pursuit of independence. Such fears were well founded. Newspapers loyal to the British occupation sought to paint Coptic participation in the revolution as a result of fear and not patriotism or solidarity. Orabi and Mustafa Kamil had both been accused previously of religious fanaticism as was the nationalist movement in the early days of 1919. As a result, Zaghloul sought to highlight Coptic participation in the Wafd both on the local level and in leadership positions. Representatives of the Wafd abroad, who were responsible for building support for the Egyptian cause, were often Copts such as Makram Ebeid, Wassef Boutros Ghali and Wissa Wassef.

Another important consideration for Zaghloul was the behavior of Copts when the nationalist movement began fragmenting as a result of differences on how to pursue the Egyptian cause. Distressed with Zaghloul's dictatorial style of leadership and his insistence on taking hard-line positions, the initial delegation, which had been expanded from seven to seventeen, began showing signs of division. The split was between Zaghloul on the one hand and his former friends from the Umma Party such as Ali Shaarawi, Abdel Aziz Fahmy, Mohamed Mahmoud and Ahmed Lutfi El Sayed. Thirteen members left the Wafd with the only ones remaining with Zaghloul being Mustafa El Nahhas and two Copts; Wassef Boutros Ghali and Sinot Hanna. At the lower levels of the party's echelons Copts, nearly unanimously, sided with Zaghloul. Remembering the role those members of the Umma

Party had played in the Egyptian Conference eight years earlier, Coptic notables trusted only Zaghloul.

The trust Zaghloul enjoyed was enormous. Only he embodied the Egyptian struggle in his person. He had managed to outmaneuver his former friends by going populist and become the undisputed leader of the nationalist movement, much to their bitterness and resentment. He was a leader Copts could rely on and swallow their fears of what an Egypt without the British would mean for them. He promised Copts complete equality and put his words into actions. With the continued arrests of leaders of the Wafd, there were moments during the 1919 revolution when the only remaining leaders outside of prison or exile were Copts. They issued the defiant declarations of the Wafd under their signatures and the masses obeyed. Sinot Hanna wrote one article after the other under the title "Nationalism is our Religion and Independence our Life." Giving a speech from the pulpit of Al Azhar Mosque, Father Sargious, a Coptic priest declared: "If the British insist on staying in Egypt under the pretence of protecting Copts, let all Copts die and Muslims live free." In 1922 the Wafd proclaimed: "There is no minority or majority in Egypt. Copts and Muslims believe in one religion, and that religion is freedom and independence." When a Copt, Youssef Wahba, was appointed as prime minister on November 21, 1919, Copts, fearful of being accused of breaking the nationalist ranks, were quick to condemn him. A meeting in the Coptic Cathedral denounced his acceptance of the position against the will of the Egyptian people. It certainly did not help that he was not viewed by Copts to be as competent as Boutros Ghali and that he had not developed strong communal ties as his predecessor had. Aghast that if Wahba were killed by a Muslim patriot it would rekindle the fire of sectarian divisions, a Copt volunteered to assassinate him. Though he survived the attempt on his life, he was forced by public pressure to resign six months later.

On February 28, 1922, Britain issued a unilateral declaration of Egyptian Independence. But it reserved four issues for its continued intervention: Sudan, British communications in Egypt, the defense of the country, and the protection of foreign interests and minorities in Egypt. While this was unacceptable to Egyptian nationalists, the process of organizing Egypt's government was nonetheless undertaken. A constitutional committee was formed to write the new Egyptian constitution, which was finally issued in April 1923. Out of thirty members, the committee included four Copts, one of whom was the church representative Metropolitan Youannes, one Syrian Catholic, and one Jew. Most of the members belonged to the former Umma Party as the Wafd had boycotted the committee with Zaghloul publically calling it "the committee of scoundrels." The debates within that committee provide important insights into how both religion in general and the Coptic question, specifically, were viewed.

The constitution addressed religion in three articles. Article 3 guaranteed non-discrimination on the basis of, among other characteristics, religion. Article 13 guaranteed freedom to practice religion, with the important exception of it disturbing public order. Article 149 declared Islam to be the nation's religion. At the time, no one objected to the last article, although the rationale for that will become clearer when discussing proportional representation. No one at the time, even Copts, imagined how the article would become a threat to their freedoms and equality.

One of the key debates among the committee members was that of proportional representation. The issue was raised by Tawfik Doss, one of the Coptic members. He proposed a system in which Copts would be selected by the general population in case not enough members of the community won seats in parliament. The rationale for his suggestion was that this closed the door on foreign intervention under the guise of protection of minorities, that the parliament was responsible for legislating in matters that affected them and thus their representation was needed, and such a system guaranteed it. Other members in the committee disagreed. They argued that such a system would destroy national unity and that it divided the nation along unnatural religious lines and not political ones.

The general public also took part in this debate with a number of newspaper articles supporting each side. The main arguments in favor were that such a division along religious lines already existed in practice in issues of personal status laws. Proponents reasoned that while they wished that such divisions were no longer relevant, in practice they were, and that the theory of equality and liberal principles should not precede reality. Christians feared a situation in the future in which they might not be elected, and reasoned that those Christians rejecting the proposal were doing so only out of fear of angering Muslims but in their hearts supported such measures. Those arguing against the suggestion, while acknowledging that religious divisions existed, claimed that they would no longer exist in the future. Religious divisions were receding with time and would finally become nonexistent. Future debates, they reasoned, would not be along sectarian lines but would be over the renaissance of Egypt.

The delusional arguments presented against the suggestion reflected the basic premises of the Umma nationalists. Due to their strong belief in the Enlightenment and the inevitable progress and evolution of man, they believed that with proper education, issues involving religion would simply cease to be relevant. They had agreed to the article declaring Islam as the religion of the state, believing it would not matter. By appeasing the religious feeling of the time, they were averting its explosion in their faces, but they were completely convinced that over time it would no longer be significant. Building a system on the very premise of the relevance of religious divisions went completely against their convictions and opened the door for religion's continued existence as politically relevant, a scenario they aimed to avoid. At the end, the motion failed, though it is worth mentioning that contrary to later historiography, Copts were in favor of it. Three Copts, including the church representative, and the Jewish member voted in favor of the suggestion, with one Copt voting against after being pressured to do so by King Fouad.[1] Outside the committee, four bishops sent telegrams with their support for the motion and so did the Coptic Milli Council and the Evangelical Milli Council. The aging pope was said to be hesitant and did not take a position on the issue, while the Wafd completely rejected the motion.

THE LIBERAL AGE AND ITS DISCONTENTS

The constitution was issued in 1923 and was soon followed by elections. While the National Party of Mustafa Kamil continued to exist, the election was fought between Saad Zaghloul and his Wafd Party, and his old friends from the Umma party who now formed the liberal constitutionalists *Al-Ahrar Al-Dostoriyoon* party. The election results were a complete endorsement of Zaghloul with his competitors winning only a few seats. With his populist demagoguery, Zaghloul had become the idol of the Egyptian masses. Zaghloul's appeal and his mobilization of the masses based on a nationalist program had allowed him to monopolize the street and use it against his enemies, foreign and domestic. His former friends were left to lick their wounds after their realization that free elections would only mean their defeat. The lesson would be understood and acted upon in the future. Holding no cards of their own, they were forced to abandon their previous democratic

---

1. The vote of the Syrian Catholic member could not be determined.

slogans and rely on more powerful players, the British or their former adversary, the king, in order to continue being part of the game. The fall of the former champions of liberalism was complete. They plotted against the Wafd when they were in the opposition, and suppressed it and organized fake elections when they reached power with the king's blessing. Never able to win the support of the masses, they used every weapon available to destroy the Wafd. In the face of its popularity, they sought to win the masses with Islam. The irony of men who were completely secular, whose own views of Islam were hardly orthodox, attempting to champion the cause of Islam against the Wafd was completely lost on them. It was only a downhill road from that point. In order to portray the Wafd as anti-Islam it was inevitable that they would involve the Copts. The Wafd was accused of being under Coptic control. The party leaders were portrayed as being under the spell of Copts and of working for Coptic interests with Copts in the Wafd becoming the favorite villains of the liberal constitutionalists' newspaper *El Siyasa*. Their true aim was to subjugate Muslims to Coptic rule, it warned, and their intention was to make Egypt Coptic. The majority was being persecuted in favor of the Coptic minority. No accusation or fabrication was off the table; no bigotry or anti-Christian slogan was beyond the pale. Anything that would destroy the Wafd was sought and championed.

The liberal constitutionalists' descent into anti-Coptic incitement continues to shock later generations of Egyptians who view them as the enlightened champions of liberalism. How could those men who had formed the very concept of the Egyptian nation, who were secular intellectuals influenced by Western civilization, who had rejected the caliphate and celebrated Egypt as a distinct entity, stoop so low? The political explanation has been the only one provided, but as this book argues, those very intellectuals, while indisputably secular, had had a Coptic problem from the very start. Their fall was not a shocking surprise but a natural development of the road they took.

The attempt to paint the Wafd as a party controlled by Copts took various forms. Saad Zaghloul's mausoleum, built like a pharaonic temple was, according to *El Siyasa,* evidence of a Coptic conspiracy. The Wafd's policy, once in power, of removing the top bureaucrats associated with its competitors from their positions, was portrayed as a Coptic plan to replace them with Copts. Every Wafdist policy was suspected of being driven by secret Coptic motives. A campaign against Copts in the Wafd was waged in *El Siyasa* and propaganda leaflets were distributed among the masses.

The attempt by the liberal constitutionalists to champion Islam and use it as a political weapon came at an appropriate moment. The end of the caliphate at the hands of Ataturk created a sense of loss and a crisis for Egyptian Muslims. Although during its last days the caliphate exercised little authority, the existence of the institution was a pillar of the Muslim world. Suddenly the political worldview of Islam was under threat. Attacks on the very concept of the caliphate by secular thinkers such as Sheikh Ali Abdel Razek, ironically from a family associated with the Liberal Constitutional Party, created the impression that Islam itself was under attack. Western scholars were attacking the foundations of Islam even in lectures inside Egypt,[2] and Egyptian scholars such as the Francophile writer Taha Hussein were echoing those criticisms.[3]

---

2. Such lectures and books critical of Islam led to denunciations in the press, especially *El Siyasa,* and after a campaign of incitement to demonstrations by students at Al Azhar.

3. The Wafd was not immune to the use of tactics involving Islam against its enemies. During the firestorm unleashed by the publication of Taha Hussein's book, *Fi Al-Shi'r Al-Gahili,* it returned the favor to the Liberal Constitutionalists. Nevertheless, whatever the failures of the Wafd during that episode, they paled in comparison to those of the Liberal Constitutionalists.

By 1928 another important development helped create this sense of crisis facing Muslims: the threat of foreign missionaries.

Foreign missionaries had been operating for many years in Egypt. In 1930, there were 450 of them freely roaming the country. With time, they had become more emboldened. In April 1928 a foreign missionary even attempted to preach Christianity inside the very center of Islamic learning, Al Azhar. Rumors of conversions of Muslims at the hand of foreign missionaries dominated the press. For Muslims, Islam had always been immune to such direct attacks. It was incomprehensible to Egyptians at the time that anyone would rationally seek to leave Islam, which was considered the superior religion. Such conversions were understood to be the result of coercion, the influence of money, or deceit. Foreign missionaries were accused of targeting the weak and vulnerable in society, especially women and the young, with their efforts. *El Siyasa* ranted that in Egypt, a country with a Muslim majority, all religions were protected except Islam. Rumors spread of children being kidnapped by missionaries in order to convert them. Articles were written warning of the threat that foreign missionary schools posed.

The Coptic Church, for its part, had an uneasy relationship with missionaries. The church viewed them as a threat to the tranquility of the situation in Egypt. Their actions were stirring Muslim anger towards Christians and that anger hardly differentiated between local Christians and foreigners, leading Copts to fear being associated with their work. For their part, the missionaries despised the Coptic Church. They viewed it not only as a traditional church that had not undergone reforms but also as having failed in converting Muslims. The work of the missionaries and their demands for the freedom to proselytize, protection for Muslim converts, and civil marriages were at best irrelevant to Copts.

The liberal constitutionalists were not the only force that attempted to use the feeling that Islam was being attacked to their advantage. The king found it expedient to be seen as the protector of Islam in face of such an onslaught. The end of the caliphate presented King Fouad, who had been chosen by the British occupation first as sultan then as king of Egypt, with a golden opportunity. With Turkey moving on a secular route, Iran as Shi'a, India too far away from the center of gravity, and the other countries in the region too weak, Fouad harbored dreams of being declared caliph of the whole Muslim world. He sought to turn his dreams into a reality by championing the cause of Islam inside Egypt and sponsoring various Islamic conferences and movements around the region to support his claims. He made sure he had a complete monopoly of Al Azhar and attempted to portray the monarchy as the protector of tradition in face of the assaults against it.

In the late '20s and early '30s, a worldwide disillusionment with liberalism and democracy was taking hold. In Latin America, populist leaders were on the rise, while in Europe totalitarian ideas were becoming more appealing. Egypt was not immune to these worldwide phenomena. The hopes of 1919 had come to naught. The Wafd would win the majority whenever free elections were held, but would soon be dismissed from office and replaced with increasingly authoritarian governments. Even when in office, the Wafd provided little for the masses who harbored idealistic dreams. The nationalist struggle against Britain had failed to win Egypt its independence. The British had not left, the king was meddling with the government, and democracy was becoming a farce. But the crisis facing Egypt was not only the failure of liberalism and democracy but more drastically the failure of modernization itself. Egypt had failed to catch up; it had paid a high price for modernization with no returns. The gap with the West was only growing and it seemed obvious that drastic measures were necessary if a remedy for the situation was to be found.

Egyptian society itself was changing. The phenomena associated with modernization were in full force. Rapid urbanization, industrialization, and mass education were taking their toll on traditional society, breaking its very foundation. This generation of Egyptians has been termed the "New *Effendis.*" They were flocking to the cities, factories, and schools with infinite dreams. Reality never met their expectations. The post-1919 order had little room for them. The lack of social and economic mobility and the closing of the political system to the 1919 generation enforced their resentment and anger with the ruling elite, political parties, and the democratic system as a whole. For some this led to a rejection of modernity itself and an attempt to return to traditional forms of organization and behavior. For others, notions of democracy and liberalism were being replaced by new totalitarian ideas emerging from Europe. To catch up, the state had to intervene forcefully in society. Political parties did nothing but fight on petty matters. Only a strong leader could save Egypt from its woes. Dictatorship had its benefits, many argued. Themes of the "just despot" became quite fashionable.

Nazi Germany and Fascist Italy became models for many. The ideological component of Nazism in the form of the race theory was naturally less popular, though it did have some adherents; but the new forms of political mobilization, propaganda, and notions of collectivism and nationalism were tremendously appealing. It was during those years that Hassan El Banna was building the first bricks of his Muslim Brotherhood and Ahmed Hussein was founding his Young Egypt. These new movements found a natural ally in the new King Farouk and his handler, Ali Maher. Maher, who despised democracy and had little faith in the people, was seeking allies for his master against the popular Wafd. For the first time, the Wafd was no longer the sole master of the street and was facing competition from these new movements. The disappointments of the '20s gave rise to the agitation of the '30s and ultimately to the turbulent '40s.

The liberal nationalists' project was set on the road to eventual doom. Elapsed now were Lutfi El Sayed's notions of Egypt's identity. Taha Hussein's conception of a Mediterranean culture to which Egypt belonged was now irrelevant. The enthusiasm for Pharaonism* born of the discovery of the Tutankhamen's tomb had fizzled away. What replaced these notions was still in formation. Japan's impressive rise gave birth to the Eastern idea, with intellectuals arguing for a bond between all Eastern peoples. The Islamism of Hassan El Banna raised the banner of an Islamic *Umma* (nation). Ahmed Hussein's Young Egypt changed the core of its nationalism as fast as it changed the movement's name with the pharaohs, the Nile, Islamism, and socialism adopted as possible foundations of the new Egypt. What was common to all of those movements was the new source of their inspiration. While indisputably modern with regard to ideas and founded along the lines of fascist movements in Europe, the new movements that came to dominate Egyptian politics were all anti-Western. The West was no longer the model to be copied, but instead the enemy to be fought. Even the realists such as Ali Maher emphasized that Egypt's destiny lay in the East. Egypt's interests, they argued, were in leading and dominating the new countries on its Eastern borders. Egypt's eyes were no longer set on Paris, but instead focused on the East.

---

* Pharaonism is an ideology that rose to prominence in Egypt in the 1920s and 1930s. It looked to Egypt's pre-Islamic past and argued that Egypt was part of a larger Mediterranean civilization.

COPTIC DISILLUSIONMENT

The Liberal Era is often portrayed as a golden age for Copts, built
on the national unity of the 1919 revolution. This reading is not
only over-simplistic, but altogether untrue. As the years went by,
the Liberal Era set the Coptic issue on a descending trajectory.
The case of Father Sargious, the Coptic orator who had in 1919
declared the death of all Copts as an adequate price for Egyptian
independence, exemplifies the descent. By 1949, Sargious was
publicly admitting his great regret at having once called for the
British to leave Egypt. Copts had cast their lot with the nationalist
struggle for independence, but independent Egypt had become
ever less hospitable to them.

The first of Coptic disappointments pertained to political
equality. When Saad Zaghloul presented his first cabinet to King
Fouad, the king was shocked to find two Copts among its ten
ministers. Commenting that this broke the tradition that allocated
only one ministry to Copts, Zaghloul famously replied that when
the British were arresting and killing Egyptians they did not
maintain a quota for Copts. Zaghloul's insistence carried the day,
but his successors were less committed to maintaining the ideals
of national unity and equality. Non-Wafdist governments gave
only one ministerial position to Copts, and with the increasing
number of portfolios, the ratio actually declined from 1 to 10, to
1 to 16, and ultimately 1 to 18. Even in its last government in 1950,
the Wafd had only one Coptic minister in an eighteen-member
cabinet.[4]

---

4. The firing of Makram Ebeid from the Wafd had affected Coptic representation in the party. Seventeen MP's followed Makram and resigned
from the Wafd. Eight of them were Copts. Due to the government commission overseeing student missions mistakenly believing him to be a Copt, he
was denied the opportunity to study abroad.

While Copts occupied some important ministries such as finance, foreign affairs, and even once defense, there were three ministries that Copts never occupied in the thirty-five successive governments that ruled Egypt between 1924 and 1952, namely interior, education and justice. These three ministries were viewed as too sensitive in possessing a religious component to their work that necessitated that they have a Muslim minister.

Coptic representation in parliament suffered a similar fate. The first parliament elected in 1924 had a Coptic membership of 7.5 percent. Rigged elections organized by anti-Wafd governments were returning parliaments with a little over 2 percent Coptic membership in the 1930s. The last Wafdist parliament in 1950 had a Coptic membership of 3 percent.

The Coptic feeling of exclusion was not limited to elected bodies. The doors to government jobs were increasingly being closed in their faces. *El Siyasa*'s campaign against Coptic civil servants was frightening Copts, and the Coptic newspaper *Masr* complained that Copts were not being promoted. Coptic complaints that certain high-ranking bureaucratic jobs were inaccessible to them continued. Positions such as school headmaster, governor, police chief, and high-ranking judicial positions were closed to them, and complaints of a quota being enforced in the police force and army were published in the Coptic press. Some Egyptian newspapers repudiated the choice of Copts as diplomats on the grounds that a Muslim nation should have Muslims as its representatives. The Egyptianization campaign in the educational sector was opening new positions to Muslims but less so to Copts as was evidenced in the case of the famed Coptic historian Aziz Suryal Atiya.[5] Equality and qualifications were not governing the choice of university

---

5. Aziz Suryal Atiya ultimately was compelled to leave Egypt and ended up at the University of Utah where he taught, founded its Middle East Center, and built one of the most impressive Middle Eastern libraries in North America. His lifelong work, the Coptic Encyclopedia, was finally published in 1991.

graduates to send on student missions to Europe, but instead an unofficial quota on Copts was enforced.[6]

Copts also continued to have problems with the public education system. Despite the fact that teaching Christianity to Coptic students was introduced by Saad Zaghloul during his time as minister of education, the problem did not cease to exist. In 1933, the Egyptian government under Ismail Sedqi decreed that teaching Islam was mandatory for Muslim students; Coptic students were free not to attend religion classes. During the '30s, the Muslim Brotherhood campaigned against allowing Copts in government schools to be taught their own religion. They argued that allowing Christianity to be taught was a propagation of Christianity. Copts were forced to build their own schools to ensure that their children were able to learn their religion. The problem was not solved until 1949 when the government finally made the teaching of religion in general mandatory, and Copts were thus allowed to study their own religion in government schools.

A more serious threat to Copts was the rise of the Muslim Brotherhood to the forefront of the political scene. One of the main reasons for founding the Brotherhood was to fight foreign missionaries and naturally Copts were lumped with them. In Banna's world, Egypt was inhabited by two kinds of people, those who summoned people to God and those who had been influenced by non-Islamic teachings. The solution to Egypt's ills was the implementation of shari'a and fighting prostitution, bars, and nudity. Rejecting Egyptian nationalism, El Banna advocated belonging to the Islamic *Umma*. In such a nation, Copts were not equal citizens; at best they were tolerated *dhimmis*. Banna argued that Copts had

---

6. Egypt's Nobel laureate Naguib Mahfouz's life changed because of such discrimination. Mahfouz, who is himself Muslim, was named after the famed Coptic medical doctor Naguib Mahfouz who delivered him as a baby. Due to the government commission overseeing student missions mistakenly believing him to be a Copt, he was denied the opportunity to study abroad.

nothing to fear from Islam because Islam asked Muslims to treat Copts well and thus guaranteed them protection. Copts however should not seek to exercise power over Muslims. It was the absolute right of the majority to enforce its laws on the land. Sinot Hanna's 1919 slogan, "Nationalism is our Religion and Independence our Life," was ridiculed. When was nationalism a religion anyway? Another slogan of the revolution, "religion is for God and the fatherland is for all," was flipped on its head. If religion was for God, then "truly the religion with God is Islam" as the Quran states, declared the Brotherhood's newspaper. Nor were Banna and his Brotherhood alone in that regard. The writer Abbas El Akkad in 1937 wrote that the utmost dream of a minority should be to be able to securely pray and not to control, allow, and forbid. Copts were to obey the majority and not try to subjugate Muslims. Ahmed Hussein, the leader of the Young Egypt Party, declared that religious tolerance should not mean that the minority is allowed to control the country or that the majority should suppress its religion to appease the minority.

Legal problems were abounding. Copts were facing restrictions in forming Coptic civil society organizations and holding religious meetings. In 1934, new regulations for the building of churches were issued. Known as the "Ten Conditions of El Ezaby Pasha," they stipulated numerous conditions and obstacles in order for a new church to be built. The most problematic conditions were the approval of Muslim inhabitants in the area in which the church was to be built, decreeing a certain space between the proposed new church and mosques, and suggesting a study of the need for a new church by determining the number of Christians in the area and the distance to the nearest church. The implementation of the ten conditions, which continues until today, has made it virtually impossible for Copts to acquire a building permit for a new church. Copts complained that Egyptian radio was discriminating against them in the amount of time allocated to broadcasting Christian rituals compared to those of Islam. In 1931, the Ministry of Justice decreed that in personal status cases, the only medical testimony accepted was that by a Muslim doctor. In 1934 a court ordered the implementation of shari'a rules in wills regardless of religion and in 1942 a fight broke over the imposition of shari'a on personal status issues involving Copts such as inheritance and divorce. On every legal front, equality for Copts was being undermined.

But more worrisome for Copts were the increasing number of attacks on them and their churches. Sheikh El Maraghi, then the sheikh of Al Azhar, and a long time ally of the Liberal Constitutionalists, had denounced Copts as "foxes" and argued that Muslims should not befriend them. The Muslim Brotherhood was distributing a book calling on Muslims to buy only from Muslim-owned shops so as to make sure that no penny falls into the hands of non-Muslims. Words soon gave way to violent actions. In March 1936, Muslims in one village objected to the building of a Coptic graveyard. In February 1938, a house that was used as a place for Christian prayer was destroyed by an angry mob. Violence toward Copts was on the rise in the form of attacking Coptic funerals, weddings, and churches, and the beating of priests. The sound of the church bell ringing was increasingly becoming provocative to Muslim neighbors. By the late '40s, the attacks on Coptic churches took a more organized and less spontaneous form. In March 1947, a church in Zagazig was burned. The following month the same fate befell a church in Alexandria and was followed by attacks on churches in Girga. The most horrific attack took place on the eve of the 1952 revolution on the January 4, 1952, in Suez. Muslim Brotherhood members burned the church and three Copts inside it. The Coptic Milli Council met two days later and declared a public mourning, announced its refusal to accept any congratulations during Coptic Christmas, and demanded the arrest and punishment of those responsible and the adoption of actions to ensure it was not repeated.[7]

The high hopes of 1919 had come crashing to the ground. Instead of ushering in a new era of harmony and equality for Copts, that era had witnessed not only the lack of a favorable closure to previous Coptic problems but also the rise of new challenges and violent attacks. The natural outcome was the erosion of Copts' confidence in the promise of a liberal Egypt and their increasing fears of what a post-British withdrawal Egypt would mean for them. Their attempts to bring their problems and complaints to the forefront of the national debate were met with utter silence or worse with a rejection of such complaints as unwelcome sectarian discourse. Copts were increasingly finding it impossible to win seats in parliament. Long gone were the days when the Wafd ran a Christian candidate in a district with very few Christians.[8]

---

7. Those actions in the form of public mourning and refusal to accept congratulations from officials were repeated again by Pope Shenouda III and the Holy Synod during their clash with Anwar Sadat in the late '70s. In 1952, Pope Shenouda, then Nazir Gayed, wrote fiery articles denouncing the attacks and demanding accountability. His actions in the '70s were greatly influenced by this earlier episode.

8. Wissa Wassef ran as a candidate of the Wafd in El Manzala district in Dakahliya, a place with very few Christians. He famously declared that "I represent in parliament a district in which there isn't a single Copt besides its MP." Wassef's statement, while celebrated by later generations as the ultimate testament to the era as a golden age, betrays the age's deficiencies. Wassef was not declaring his identity in that statement, nor celebrating it. He was in fact declaring the other party's, the Muslims', identity, whose tolerance was being celebrated. The other famous quote from that era, that of Makram Ebeid, "I am a Copt by religion, while a Muslim by citizenship," suffers from the same deficiency. Ebeid who was more conscious and politically ambitious than Wassef, betrayed in his statement the fact that he was forced to shed his identity in order to belong.

THE CHURCH IN TURMOIL

The Coptic historian Iris Habib El Masry titled the sixth volume of her book *The Story of the Coptic Church*, which covers the popes that followed Kyrillos V, *How Have the Mighty Fallen?* While El Masry is hardly an impartial observer of that period given the role her father played in the intra-church disputes, her title is quite appropriate. Pope Kyrillos V was followed by three popes who had been bishops/metropolitans and sought to occupy the papal throne in a serious breach of church tradition. For centuries the Coptic Church had insisted on maintaining the tradition of monks being elevated to the papacy. Unlike in the Roman Catholic Church, the papacy according to Coptic Orthodox theology is not a position above bishops, but the pope, by virtue of being the bishop of Alexandria, is merely considered as first among equals. Since bishops are considered married for life to their dioceses and Christianity does not endorse divorce nor does it accept polygamy by taking a second wife, a bishop cannot marry the diocese of Alexandria and in so doing become pope. The breaking of this tradition ignited a storm of controversy that overshadowed the reign of the three popes. Unlike monks, who by virtue of their seclusion in the monasteries are not likely to initiate a media and organizational campaign to win the papacy, bishops were powerful figures who had at their disposal various means to secure the nomination. The papal elections and the intra-church fights threatened the institution of the church and left it and the Coptic community deeply wounded.

Pope Youannes XIX (r. 1928–1942) was born in 1858. At the age of seventeen he entered the monastery and in 1887 was chosen as metropolitan* of Behira. He had quickly risen to become

---

* A title within the rank of bishops used by the Coptic Church.

Kyrillos V's right hand man. His tasks were numerous. He was made responsible for the monasteries of the Baramos and Saint Bishoy, as well as overseeing the diocese of Monofia after the death of its bishop, and was chosen as the pope's representative in Alexandria. He took part in Kyrillos's battles with the Milli Council and shared his short banishment in 1892. Known as a conservative in church affairs, he was viewed as the archenemy of the Milli Council and the defender of the monasteries' right to control their endowments, making him the church establishment's favorite candidate to succeed Kyrillos V.

The Holy Synod convened in July 1928 and agreed that bishops could be nominated to the papacy. King Fouad was in favor of Youannes's election. In his attempt to counter the popularity of the Wafd, the king had sought to become the defender of religious institutions in Egypt. Although a few names were suggested, the anti-Youannes Copts never managed to nominate a heavyweight to run against him and were divided among themselves. Youannes's main competitor was a monk serving in Sudan who was rumored to be close to the British occupation there and was thus viewed unfavorably by nationalists. His cause was not helped by the fact that before becoming a monk he had been married, making his candidacy another break with church tradition. King Fouad engineered Youannes's elevation to the papacy by limiting the voting pool to ninety-six individuals who were then informed of the king's wish to see Youannes elected. When elections were held on December 16, 1928 the results were guaranteed. Youannes was elected as the 113th pope of Alexandria with seventy votes.

As locum tenens before his elevation to the papacy, Youannes had attempted to win over his detractors by promising to support reform efforts of the church. He had ordered that monks return to their monasteries, that priests be selected only from graduates of the theological seminary to improve their quality, and most

importantly proposed a joint commission to oversee the endowments, half of whose members were to be chosen from the Milli
Council and the other half from the Holy Synod. This last promise
would haunt him throughout his papacy with public anger mounting against him because the promise was never kept. Youannes
XIX's reign, like that of his predecessor, was spent fighting the
Milli Council over control of the church finances. The council
attempted to take control of the endowments and refused to pay
the salaries of those working in the papacy which forced the pope
to seek government funds in order to maintain a functioning
papacy.

Pope Youannes nonetheless managed to open a school for
monks in 1929 that would help elevate the quality of their education, as well as organize the libraries of the monasteries. During
his reign, Morcos Semika collected Coptic antiques and organized
them into a Coptic Museum. In 1931, the government took control of the museum leading to a conflict with the church. Youannes
was the third pope in the history of the Coptic Church to visit
Ethiopia and continued to play the role of diplomat for the
Egyptian state as his predecessors had. Faced with attacks and
insults by the Milli Council, Youannes came to regret his decision
to seek the papacy declaring, "I wish the day had been doomed
when I sought the papacy."

Metropolitan Yusab of Girga was selected locum tenens following Pope Youannes's death in 1942. The election of the new
pope pitted two strong candidates from among the bishops against
one another. Yusab was the favorite of the conservative establishment, while partisans of reform backed Metropolitan Macarius of
Asyut. Few raised their voices against the reiteration of the aban-
donment of tradition by elevating a bishop to the post, with the
most notable exception being Habib El Masry, Iris's father. When
elections were held, Macarius secured the nomination with 1,221

votes to Yusab's 736 votes and 349 divided among four other candidates.

Pope Macarius III (r. 1942–1945) was born in 1872. Joining the monastery at the age of sixteen, he was selected for the diocese of Asyut in 1897. As metropolitan of Asyut, Macarius was known as a champion of reform. He had given control over the endowments in his diocese to the local Milli Council and had established a large library and a number of schools. Responsible for Asyut, the center of the Protestant missionary work, he was remarkably favorably disposed towards the missionaries and, unlike the rest of the church establishment, cooperated with them. Also, unlike the rest of the church establishment, he endorsed the Coptic Conference and spoke at its opening ceremony. Given this reputation, the Milli Council was under the impression that it had finally won the battle against the clergy. The pope was a reformer and the council believed that he would initiate a period of tranquility and cooperation for the benefit of the community. Nothing could have been further from the truth.

Pope Macarius III certainly began his papacy with the intention of cooperating with the council. Upon being enthroned he gave them control over all endowments including those of the monasteries. His action predictably angered the bishops who gathered the Holy Synod against his will and denounced his decision. But if the pope thought his battle would be only with the bishops he was wrong. Only a few months passed before he clashed with the Milli Council. The council was again overplaying its hand and attempting to subject the clergy to its control. The pope's clash with the council resulted in him moving closer to his bishops and mending his relations with them. Frustrated and depressed by his fight with the council and their attacks on him, he moved to a monastery and refused to return to his seat. Upon arriving in the proximity of the monastery, he insisted on walking to its gates kneeling along the way in what observers described as a pilgrimage of repentance. He was heard cursing himself in his prayers: "I sinned when I became patriarch. May I become handicapped or blind." Though he later returned to Cairo due to appeals from the community, he was a broken man. He never consecrated any bishops during his reign and prayed for his own death. His papacy lasted less than two years.

The fate of his two predecessors had little effect on Yusab who once again sought the papacy. There was a drive by some members of the Milli Council to cancel the law requiring the celibacy of the candidates for the papacy and to nominate a member of the laity. The bishops, for their part, insisted again that the pope be chosen from among their ranks. Wadie Saeed, a university graduate known for his piety, had become a monk under the name of Daoud El Makary in the interim before the selection of the new pope and became the favorite candidate of those championing the revival efforts of the church. The Holy Synod responded by refusing to recognize his monastic vows and thus disqualifying him. Yusab, like Pope Youannes, attempted to appease his detractors and won over the partisans of the Milli Council. After an election in which the leaders of the council secured army transportation for their supporters on a day that had witnessed a transportation workers' strike, Yusab won the papacy in May 1946.

Pope Yusab II (r. 1946–1956) was born in 1875. As a monk he had been sent by Kyrillos V to Athens to study theology and was chosen as the metropolitan of Girga in 1929. His honeymoon with the Milli Council was short-lived after he refused to hand them control of the endowments. The Milli Council at the time was led by Ibrahim Fahmy El Minyawey and his main supporter, Father Ibrahim Louka. Both men had little interest in the revival aspect of the Coptic Church. Ibrahim Louka was often accused of being close to the British occupation authorities. The truth of the accusation notwithstanding, he was certainly much enchanted with Protestantism and close to Egypt's Anglican Church. Uninterested in the work of Habib Guirguis and those who sought to rediscover and emphasize Orthodox theology, he sought to reform the Coptic Church along Protestant lines. He attempted to appoint an Anglican priest as a teacher of Greek in the Coptic Theological Seminary and sent Copts to study theology in Britain.

The rupture between the revivalists and the Milli Council was complete. Like their predecessors at the time of Pope Kyrillos V, the revivalists were staunchly Orthodox. They were not antagonistic to the idea of reforming the Coptic Church. In fact they championed such calls. But their notion of reform was quite specific. They did not seek the destruction of the church institution but its reform. Their solution to the plight of Coptic teaching was a return to the roots of the Coptic Church in order for it to be able to defend itself against the Protestant missionaries. They supported and used modern methods and education but their goal was a reemphasis on what made the Coptic Church unique. The supporters and members of the Milli Council who called themselves reformers had a different agenda. Completely modern in outlook, they had little interest and less passion in the historical roots and unique character of the Coptic Church. Captivated by the Protestant ethic and outlook, their ultimate goal was to reform the Coptic Church along the lines of the Protestant Reformation. Their solution to the miserable state of the Coptic Church was the removal of the clergy from control of church affairs and the handing of the leadership of the community to the laity, making them its natural leaders. While both camps shared a strong displeasure at the current state of the Coptic Church and were strongly opposed by the conservative traditionalist clergy, their own battles against each other were no less fierce.

Some of those depressed by the state of the Coptic Church channeled their passion in Coptic civil society organizations. The 1940s witnessed a flourishing of such groups. Some focused on helping the needy, others at establishing orphanages and caring for the young. The Coptic Women's Organization for the Upbringing of Children managed to establish fifty-one new schools between 1940 and 1952. Magazines dedicated to Coptic themes were widespread. Led by Aziz Suryal Atiya (1898–1988), Sami Gabra (1898–1979), and Mourad Kamil (1908–1957), those seeking the revival of the Coptic Church's roots established the Institute of Coptic Studies in 1954. An outstanding educational institution, it helped preserve and revive the Coptic language, Coptic music, and Coptic iconography and established disciplines in diverse fields such as African studies and archaeology. In 1927, Ragheb Moftah (1898–2001) began his seventy-year work on documenting and preserving Coptic music and liturgy. Merrit Boutros Ghali started a society dedicated to Coptic archaeology. The revival of the Coptic language was not ignored with considerable efforts dedicated to that end. Habib Guirguis continued his fifty-year work in the Coptic Theological Seminary producing more educated and knowledgeable priests and preachers.

No matter how much those efforts attempted to overcome it by focusing on civil society, the internal crisis of the Coptic Church could not be ignored. Accompanying Pope Yusab to the papacy was his valet and assistant Malak Guirguis. Malak, an illiterate man who had managed to become indispensible to the pope during his time in Girga, came to completely dominate the aging pope. Rumors of the practice of simony by Malak began circulating and were soon confirmed. To obtain any church position, Malak had to be paid. Anger was mounting inside the lay community, the council, and the bishops.

The first to channel its anger into action was a group called the Society of the Coptic Nation. The group shared certain organizational aspects with the Muslim Brotherhood leading many to describe it as a Coptic response to the Brotherhood's rise. In reality the group was much shallower and less successful than its Muslim counterpart. Established in September 1951, the group called for being governed by the Bible and committed its members to speaking Coptic. On July 25, 1954, members of the group entered the patriarchal residence, and awakening the aging pope, threatened to shoot him if he did not sign a renunciation of his position. Frightened, the pope signed and was taken to a nunnery. The members then occupied the papal residence and announced their action to the world, demanding that the new revolutionary government in Egypt not interfere in internal church affairs. The standoff lasted for four days until the government moved in and arrested the thirty-six men who had occupied the residence.

Two months later it was the turn of the Holy Synod to take action. Angered by the widespread corruption and demanding reform, the Holy Synod met despite the pope's refusal on September 25, 1954. They demanded that the pope banish Malak from his service and appoint a committee composed of three bishops to assist the pope in managing the church's affairs. After initially refusing to agree to their demands and excommunicating them, the pope finally relented and verbally agreed to their demands on October 7. The pope's agreement was however in name only and nothing changed.

One year later, after a bishop clashed with Malak, the pope ordered the bishop removed from his responsibilities in overseeing a monastery's endowments. That was the last straw for the Holy Synod. The Holy Synod met and ordered that the pope be relieved from his duties in managing the church. He was given the opportunity to choose a monastery for his exile and he travelled to the Monastery of the Virgin Mary (*Al Muhharaq*). Both the Milli Council, which had lost all its importance due to Nasser's policies, and the government, endorsed the decision. However the church in Ethiopia rejected the decision on November 28, 1955, and refused to acknowledge the authority of the three bishops tasked with managing the church's affairs.

A year later, with passions cooling down, Pope Yusab, relying on the support of the Ethiopian bishops, held a meeting of the Holy Synod in the monastery on June 20, 1956. The synod was attended by seven Ethiopian and thirteen Egyptian bishops, while the majority of the Egyptian bishops refused to attend. In the meeting, the pope agreed to relieve Malak of his service and the bishops endorsed his return to Cairo and the papacy. The rest of the bishops rejected the decision.

The situation was about to explode. The aging pope returned to Cairo on June 24, 1956, and attempted to enter the patriarchy. He found the doors chained and people shouting insults at him. Violence might start at any second. He went to the Coptic Hospital where his health collapsed. On his deathbed, he was carried to the patriarchy where he was allowed entrance to die on his throne. He died less than twenty-four hours later on November 13, 1956.

Why had Kyrillos V so brilliantly succeeded in his struggles against the Milli Council while his successors suffered so much? Unlike Kyrillos, who enjoyed the near unanimous support of the clergy, the struggle between bishops to occupy the papacy had left them deeply divided and unable to take a common stand. The breaking of church tradition by elevating them to the papacy had alienated the traditionalists, and their campaigns to win the seat had led to mutual attacks on one another. Kyrillos V's piety and personal virtue was never in doubt, while Yusab's conduct left a lot to be desired. While hardly a modernizer, Kyrillos had enjoyed the support of those seeking the revival of the Coptic Church especially that of his deacon Habib Guirguis, while Yusab had no admirers. Also important was the fact that Kyrillos's most violent clash with the Milli Council in 1892 came eighteen years after his assumption of the papacy, which had allowed him ample time to consolidate his control of the institution.

One important development that occurred during this period is worth elaboration: the relationship between the Coptic Church and its Ethiopian daughter. Ever since the fourth century, an Egyptian monk had been consecrated as metropolitan of Ethiopia. While some of those chosen were certainly pious men, others were less qualified. The language barrier and ignorance of the customs of the land were certainly tremendous obstacles for all those selected. With the spread of Christianity in the land and the growth of its population, the responsibilities of bishop became too much for any one man to bear. Kyrillos V had been asked by the Ethiopian emperor to consecrate one metropolitan and four bishops, to which he agreed. Emperor Haile Selassie (1892–1975) was keen on consolidating his authority and establishing imperial control over the Ethiopian Church. With the number of Ethiopian Christians far surpassing that of Copts and Ethiopia being an independent country while Copts were a mere minority in Egypt, it was but natural that Ethiopians would seek to redress the balance in the relationship between the two churches and gain a form of independence.

In 1929, the emperor succeeded in gaining Pope Youannes's approval for the consecration of an Egyptian metropolitan and four Ethiopian bishops for the first time. During the Italian occupation of Ethiopia and Haile Selassie's exile, the Egyptian

metropolitan rejected Italian demands to secede from the Coptic
Church and, as a result, was banished to Egypt. In 1937, the Italians declared the independence of the Ethiopian Church, giving
it a patriarch and thirteen bishops, a move that was condemned
by the Coptic Church and led to those men's excommunication.
Upon his return to Ethiopia, Emperor Haile Selassie was determined to win the Ethiopian Church's autonomy. After long negotiations and appeals, he finally won in 1946 his key demand of the
consecration of an Ethiopian metropolitan once the Egyptian
one, who was not allowed to exercise his power and remained in
Egypt, had died. However, afraid that it might lead to the complete separation of the two churches, the Coptic Church refused
to grant this metropolitan the right to consecrate bishops. During
the negotiations the Egyptian government heavily pressured the
church to assent to Ethiopian demands because of Egyptian interests in water projects on the Nile.

   In 1948, Pope Yusab further agreed to the right of the future
Ethiopian metropolitan to consecrate bishops on his own and in
the interim before the Egyptian metropolitan's death, consecrated
five Ethiopian bishops thus achieving the Ethiopian Church's
autocephaly. They were all required to swear to maintain the
Orthodox faith and loyalty to the mother church in Egypt. In
1951, after the death of the last Egyptian metropolitan, Abuna
Basilios was consecrated by Pope Yusab as the first Ethiopian
metropolitan. Yusab's acquiescence with Ethiopian demands made
him a hero in their eyes and ensured that he enjoyed their support
during his future troubles. The relationship between the churches
again soured with negotiations continuing until Pope Kyrillos VI
agreed to all Ethiopian demands and in 1959 consecrated Abuna
Basilios as Patriarch Catholicos. The 1976 decision by the communist government in Ethiopia to remove the Ethiopian Patriarch

Tewophilos from his seat, which was rejected by the Coptic Church, would cut all ties between the two churches. Today the two churches enjoy a cordial relationship grounded on equality with the Ethiopian Church recognizing the supremacy in honor of the Coptic pope.

CHAPTER SEVEN

Pharaohs and Titans

AND THEN THERE WAS NASSER

T HE OFFICIAL COLLAPSE of the Egyptian regime came on July 23, 1952, when a small clique of Army officers known as the Free Officers and led by Colonel Gamal Abdel Nasser, was able to move its troops to take control of key government locations. In reality however, the regime had collapsed a long time before that. The end of World War II had ushered in an era of agitation by the Muslim Brotherhood and Young Egypt. The Palestine War in 1948 had destroyed whatever remaining legitimacy the system had. Failed attempts at winning independence through negotiations with the British and an appeal to the United Nations had only added fuel to the fire. A wave of violence and political assassinations took the lives of two prime ministers and Hassan El Banna. A brief moment of enthusiasm with the return of the Wafd to power in 1950 came to nothing. Attacks on British forces in the Suez Canal zone ended with a violent confrontation between them and Egyptian interior ministry forces and the next day the burning of Cairo.

The men who formed the Free Officers conspiracy belonged to the generation known as the new effendis. They had become disillusioned with the Wafd and parliamentary democracy in general. They had joined the new movements that emerged during the '30s from the Muslim Brotherhood to Young Egypt, and some of them were enchanted by leftist ideas and communist organizations. Some of them collaborated with the Nazis, others took part in various earlier conspiracies and assassinations. Their ideas and ideologies had not yet matured, but they shared a belief in the necessity of revolutionary change, an anti-liberal and anti-democratic disposition, and a strong belief in the state as a means of change, social engineering, and ultimately modernization.

After an initial honeymoon with the Muslim Brotherhood, the clash between the Free Officers and their former allies became unavoidable. Winner-takes-all politics allowed no room for two strong competing groups to share power in Egypt. By 1954, the Free Officers had crushed their opponents and cleansed their own ranks. Nasser emerged as the undisputed leader. Egypt was about to embark on a different course, a course that would bring it much sorrow.

Nasser adopted pan-Arabism, but his Arab nationalism was not the same as that of the Baathists in the Levant. Pan-Arabism for Egypt was a device of realism. Before 1952 Egypt had not viewed itself as Arab. Its new passion for the cause was a means of attaining primacy. By championing the Arab cause of unity and the liberation of Palestine, Nasser had become larger than the country he ruled. For Copts, the new identity was a further erosion of their distinct uniqueness. Unlike the Arab Christians of the Levant, Copts never viewed themselves as Arabs and never developed a passion for the delusion of unity. Copts also had little enthusiasm for Nasser's anti-Western inclinations and less so for his animosity towards Israel. While hardly friendly towards Jews due to a long-standing theological animosity and the historical competition between them as minorities in the service of Muslim rulers, Copts had little fervor for a conflict that they viewed, at best, as irrelevant to Egypt's interests.

Internally, Nasser consolidated the power of the Egyptian state. Civil society fell victim to a mindset that did not consider any aspect of life independent of the state or immune to state intervention. The great flourishing of Coptic civil society organizations in the '40s came to a sudden halt. Party politics was another victim. While Nasser ultimately failed to build a coherent party capable of mobilizing the masses—his relationship with the masses who worshiped him allowed no go-betweens—the erosion of meaningful political participation meant the collapse of a whole class in Egyptian society. Copts were especially hurt by these policies. Though they complained of a lack of equal representation before the revolution, Copts had had at least some representation. The old ruling class was replaced by a new one composed of army officers and, with minimal representation in the military, Copts were suddenly without any representative. Faced with a situation where no Copt was elected to the Egyptian Parliament, Nasser first tested the possibility of closing some districts to only Coptic candidates. When that proved unworkable, he attempted to solve the problem by appointing some Copts to parliament by presidential decree. Those appointed were naturally not true representatives of the community but merely technocrats with no real authority, as were the few Coptic ministers who successively served in Nasser's governments. Coptic representation became completely dependent on Nasser's goodwill. The government's expansion in the economic sphere, while not driven by any sectarian intention, nonetheless meant increased room for discrimination. Coptic representation in the newly established and confiscated economic enterprises was at a bare minimum and so was their representation in the diplomatic service. Nasser did not appoint a single Copt as ambassador and the percentage of Copts in government service steadily declined.

Nasser's socialist policies also proved quite detrimental to the Coptic community. As the doors to government service had narrowed for them before 1952, Copts had increasingly resorted to private enterprise. Now nationalization policies resulted in a disproportionate erosion of Coptic wealth. Nasser's confiscation of large landholdings further heightened their plight. While both Christians and Muslims were affected by those confiscations, the land was overwhelmingly redistributed to Muslims.

However, Nasser's educational and religious policies were to prove the most worrisome in the long run. While Nasser was certainly a secular man, his education minister, Kamal El Din Hussein was not. Hussein, who had belonged to the Brotherhood before he joined the Free Officers conspiracy, certainly harbored Islamist inclinations. Under his leadership, the Egyptian educational system was Islamized step by step. Arabic textbooks became more and more indistinguishable from religious ones. Instead of literary texts, students were now required to memorize parts of the Quran for their Arabic language exams. The poems taught were ones praising the Prophet. More emphasis was also put on religious teaching with religion becoming a pass or fail subject for students. Faced with a challenge from the Muslim Brotherhood, Nasser attempted to monopolize religion. The state provided lavishly for Al Azhar and a huge expansion in religious education took place. Such spending was for an institution that naturally provided only for Muslims.

But in other areas, Copts gained from Nasser's policies. His crackdown on the Muslim Brotherhood removed a threat to Copts, though that crushing would prove only temporarily under his successors. As an institution, the Coptic Church greatly benefited from Nasser's policies. His destruction of the old ruling elite meant the removal of the clergy's historical enemy: the Milli Council proponents. Nasser's confiscation of land included that of religious endowments. On September 21, 1955, he also abolished religious courts. With those two decisions, the reasons for conflict between clergy and leaders of the laity were removed. In fact, the very reason for the council's existence had been abolished. No new elections for a Milli Council took place after 1961 to the great joy of the conservative religious establishment.

Nasser did not hold any personal animosity towards Christians. He was simply not interested in the church. He had much larger concerns beyond Egypt's borders than such petty matters. For him, forging a good relationship with the church leadership was enough. To that end, Nasser and Pope Kyrillos VI managed to find a working bond. Nasser deferred to the pope in all matters concerning Copts including their appointment to parliament. The pope in turn supported Nasser both in general policies, such as the Coptic Church's rejection of Vatican II's *Nostra Aetate* language on absolving Jews of the blood of Christ, and in Nasser's hour of need when he resigned after his 1967 defeat. Nasser's iron-fist control did not allow any mob violence to be directed towards Copts or their churches. His friendly relationship with the pope allowed him to contribute financially to the building of the new St. Mark Cathedral which became the papal headquarters. He personally participated in laying its foundation as well as its opening and the celebrations that accompanied the return of parts of the relics of St. Mark to Egypt. Pope Kyrillos's deep spirituality, which had a profound impact on Emperor Haile Selassie, allowed Nasser to use this connection in favor of Egypt's relationship with Ethiopia. When the Virgin Mary appeared in Zeitoun in 1968, Nasser was rumored to have personally gone to see the appearance.

THE GIANT AND THE FOUNDING FATHERS

The seeds that Habib Guirguis had planted in the church through the theological seminary and the Sunday schools were beginning to grow into a strong movement that was soon to take the church by storm. Their ascendency was neither preordained nor smooth but was met with fierce resistance both by the church's old guard and by the lay leaders of the community. However, through their own inner strength and the guiding hand and protection of an unlikely figure, they ultimately triumphed.

In the late '30s and early '40s a new generation had been drawn to the church. They were not illiterate adherents who followed the clergy blindly, but instead some of the best minds Egypt had to offer. They were the products of the modern education system, middle-class university graduates from all fields—engineers, medical doctors, and pharmacists—people who had bright careers ahead of them, yet their hearts and minds were drawn to the Coptic Church. They had no doubt that it was theirs and that they had a duty towards it. They abandoned bright futures and chose the deserts of Egypt and its nearly abandoned churches to launch their revolution.

Their goal was the revival of their church and returning it to its old glory. Confronted by the traditions and rules of the old clergy, they claimed an older and more venerable tradition. They embraced the ethos of the early years of the church; the days in which the light of Alexandria shone throughout the world were their model. Faced with fierce opposition by priests and bishops they raised the banners of St. Anthony, St. Athanasius, and St. Cyril. They were not political manipulators who used a historical mythology to gain control. They were firm believers who aimed to change the church from within.

The Sunday School Movement was born in four churches in Greater Cairo. The geographical division soon gave way to an ideological one as well. Two schools emerged as the models for the revival, others fell under their guidance. The first was that of St. Mark's Church in Giza and was led by Saad Aziz (who would later become Bishop Samuel), Yassa Hanna, and Wahib Suryal (Father Salib Suryal). In the face of tremendous poverty in the villages of Giza those young church servants visited, they developed a clear social consciousness. They emphasized a Christian message that went beyond just bringing the message of the Gospel to poor village Christians. Along with the words of Christ, they brought his material blessings—whatever their small resources could manage. They excelled in Bible studies and emphasized an understanding of God's message as a means to revival. They sought to recruit educated laymen to the clergy. Zarif Abdallah was the first to become a priest under the name of Father Boulos Boulos. Others soon followed. Wives were found overnight to fulfill the requirement that priests marry.[1]

The other school was in St. Anthony Church in Shubra. Its star was Nazir Gayed, who would become Pope Shenouda III. The St. Anthony School stressed spiritual revival. Emphasis was put on prayer as a means to God. What the church needed the most was an inner discovery of Christ. The St. Anthony group frowned upon the social activism of Giza as a diversion from the true mission. Some labeled those in Giza as Protestant, the term not intended as a compliment.

The lines were not always sharply drawn. Nazir Gayed had an all-encompassing view of the role of the church. Youssef Iskandar (Father Matta El Meskeen) was personally very ecumenical in spirit and open to cooperation with Protestants. Abdel Messih Bishara (Bishop Athanasius) though from a third group in St. Mary's Church in Fagallah, would ultimately become Saad Aziz's most

---

1. Unlike the Catholic Church, the Coptic Church insisted that its priests be married. The logic was that the role of priests in serving in the world naturally meant dealing with all aspects of human problems and that leading a normal life and raising a family made them more capable of dealing with such issues.

brilliant follower. Kamal Habib (Bishop Bimen) was a church servant in Giza, but also one of those who followed Father Matta El
Meskeen. In the end it was the internal divisions among those
who stressed the internal spiritual revival which would prove to be
the longest standing.

They were continually involved in battles on all fronts. Bishops
and priests threw them out of their churches as they viewed them
as competitors. Local Milli Councils opposed them as they were
regarded as wasting church resources. They stood their ground.
Kicked out of one church, they went to another. The ultimate irony
was that as members of the laity they were more dedicated to the
church than its old clergy. They visited the old monasteries for
retreats, seeking spiritual renewal. In due course, their stays there
became permanent. The lives of the early hermits of the fourth and
fifth centuries had captivated them. Youssef Iskandar and Saad
Aziz were the first to become monks in 1948; others soon followed. Only one monastery, the Virgin Mary El Sorian, was open
to them. Other bishops and abbots of monasteries were suspicious
of these young men, but Bishop Theophilus of El Sorian welcomed
those university graduates.

In 1957 the doors of the papacy were wide open. Enthusiasm
swept the community as 5,500 registered to vote in the new papal
elections in Cairo. With three votes each, 5,400 of the registrants
nominated Father Matta El Meskeen (Youssef Iskandar), 5,300
Father Makary El Soriany (Saad Aziz)[2] and 5,200 Antonious

---

2. Upon becoming a monk a person is given a new name. His new first
name is that of a saint. The second half of his name is that of the monastery
he belongs to. Thus Makary El Soriany means "Monk Macarius of the Monastery of the Virgin Mary the Syrian." Upon being consecrated bishop, a new
name is chosen. Hence Saad Aziz became Makary El Soriany in 1948 and in
1962 Bishop Samuel.

El Soriany (Nazir Gayed). The old bishops and members of the Milli Council were horrified. The Sunday school servants were now in the footsteps of the throne of St. Mark's successor. In their panic, the clergy and old elite ran to the state. They changed the nomination rules for candidates. The new government decree issued on November 3, 1957, and still in effect today limited the number of voters to a small category controlled by bishops and stipulated that candidates for the papal seat had to be a minimum forty years old and to have spent at least fifteen years as monks. The old bishops thought that by this measure they had avoided the bullet. Of course, while successful in keeping the young monks away from the papacy this time around, the rules would prove meaningless in the long run. Faced with deep anger in the community, the locum tenens at the time sought to reach out to them by putting the name of the young monks' confession father, Mina El Baramousy, up for nomination. When elections were held, Father Mina barely made it coming in third place in the number of votes. But God had another plan in mind. When a blindfolded child picked one of the three papers put on the altar,[3] the name written on it was that of Mina El Baramousy.

---

3. The process by which Coptic popes are selected is a complex one. The Holy Synod and Milli Council members nominate candidates and a select committee of them dismisses those deemed unqualified or objected to by petitions from the community. Five to seven candidates remain and are put forward to a vote by a small category of monks, priests, members of local Milli Councils and other Coptic notables. In the last election in 2012, 2,412 individuals had the right to vote. Voters can choose three candidates and the three candidates with the highest number of votes then move to the final process. After prayers and fasting for three days by the whole community, a blindfolded altar boy picks one of the three papers with the candidates' names. The logic behind the complex process is to benefit from all forms of selection: qualification (Holy Synod nominations), popular will (elections) and, finally, heavenly choice through the hand of the blindfolded child.

Azer Youssef Atta (Father Mina El Baramousy) was born in 1902. After finishing high school he worked in the private sector. In 1927 he left the world for the Baramous Monastery, becoming a monk a year later. After studying in the Monks School in Helwan, he asked for permission in 1933 to live in seclusion in the desert. Living for a time in an abandoned windmill, his holiness and spirituality soon attracted the young Sunday school servants. In a church in crisis that seemed to have hit rock bottom, his deep piety shone as a star in a dark night. Made responsible for the abandoned monastery of St. Samuel the Confessor, he sent Saad Aziz and Youssef Iskandar there and later to El Sorian Monastery.

He chose the name Kyrillos VI (r. 1959–1971). The task placed on his shoulders was enormous. The scandals of the church during the reign of Yusab II were still fresh in people's minds. He had to keep a tough balance between the young reformers and the old bishops who viewed them and him with suspicion. He moved cautiously. He removed the papal entourage that controlled previous popes. His doors were open to any member of the community who wished to visit him. Unlike previous popes who kept the protocol of receiving visitors but did not venture forth to visit others, he visited churches and people across the country. His profound spirituality left a deep mark on Emperor Haile Selassie and mended the ties with Ethiopia which he visited. He supported the efforts of Father Makary El Soriany in opening the Coptic Church to the rest of Christianity. As a monk he had forged a spiritual bond with the fourth century St. Menas and dreamed of reviving the area in the desert close to Alexandria in which he had lived. Beginning in 1959, he laid the foundations of what would become a great monastery in the area. Seeking to celebrate nineteen centuries of Christianity in Egypt and the martyrdom of St. Mark, he sought and was granted by the Vatican a small part of St. Mark's relics.

The return of part of the relics of St. Mark to Egypt in June 1968 was an occasion of great joy and immense celebrations by Copts and their Church. The relics were buried under the grand cathedral Kyrillos built in Cairo, which became the headquarters of the papacy in Egypt.

On September 30, 1962, Pope Kyrillos consecrated Makary El Soriany and Antonious El Soriany as general bishops. The move was unprecedented. Up to that time, the Coptic Church had only had bishops consecrated to serve a geographical diocese. By consecrating them as general bishops, he was able to include the young monks in the Holy Synod without completely alienating the old guard. Makary El Soriany became Bishop Samuel who was responsible for ecumenical and social services while Antonious El Soriany became Bishop Shenouda, responsible for the theological seminary and church upbringing. In 1967 he consecrated the third general bishop, Gregorious, for the Institute of Coptic Studies. The young Sunday school servants had reached the center of power in the Coptic Church. These were the Founding Fathers and the story of the Coptic Church since has been the story of these men and their competing views.

Bishop Samuel was the star of the Giza Sunday School Movement. Born in 1920, he obtained a law degree at the age of nineteen, and then studied at the American University in Cairo. He volunteered in Ethiopia as a Sunday school teacher. The most dynamic and vibrant leader of the Sunday School Movement in Giza, he was one of the two first university graduates to become monks in 1948. As a monk, Makary El Soriany had broken the historical isolation of the Coptic Church. Together with the great historian Aziz Suryal Atiya and Father Salib Suryal, he represented the Coptic Church at the 1954 World Council of Churches meeting held in Illinois. Impressed with his character and deep commitment to ecumenicalism, Princeton University granted him a scholarship and he received his M.A. in sociology there. His life can be summed up in two words: ecumenicalism and social work. As bishop of social services, he oversaw the tremendous growth of the Coptic Church in providing services to the community. He opened vocational training centers, distributed vaccinations in isolated villages, provided medical aid to the needy and literacy classes to the elderly. No area was closed to his passion and hard work. Centers for drug addicts were built, the mentally handicapped were cared for, and he even established places for girls who had become pregnant out of wedlock. He founded a project to help the garbage collectors in Cairo. For him, leading a good Christian life meant work with and for the needy. "Love thy neighbor" was his working philosophy. He used his extensive connections abroad to secure funding for his activities and did not shy away from taking money from Protestant churches in the United States and Europe. When Egypt was in its darkest hour after the 1967 war, it was Bishop Samuel who was able to secure necessary medical equipment for the country. He was the founder of the first Coptic churches in the West.

Bishop Shenouda, born in 1923, was a completely different man in character and disposition. A poet, who served in the army as a conscript during the 1948 Palestine War, he had been involved in Egyptian politics before becoming a monk and kept this interest all his life. In 1946, he had been one of the leaders of the Sunday School Movement in St. Anthony Church in Shubra. After graduating from university with a degree in history, he studied at the theological seminary and upon graduation in 1949 began teaching there. He became the editor of the Sunday school magazine and used it as a means to attack the church establishment and call for reform.

His confession father was Matta El Meskeen, and in 1954 he joined him in El Sorian Monastery as a monk, taking the name

Antonious El Soriany. He followed Matta El Meskeen in leaving the monastery in 1956 and going to St. Samuel Monastery. There, under the harsh conditions the two men clashed. He returned to El Sorian Monastery shortly thereafter and then lived as a hermit in the desert.

As a bishop he opened the doors to his lectures in the theological seminary to the whole Coptic community. His weekly sermons, which became a popular attraction, were not solely devoted to spiritual themes. He received and answered questions about everything and provided spiritual answers for every aspect of life. The church, for him, could not be isolated from its surroundings. It had to address everything and defend the collective rights of Copts. He established *Al Keraza* magazine and was its editor-in-chief until his death in 2011. His fiery sermons, headiness, and lack of willingness to accept criticism soon brought him in conflict with the Institute for Coptic Studies, Bishop Samuel, whom he greatly disliked, and eventually Pope Kyrillos VI. In 1967 Pope Kyrillos consecrated his old mentor Wahib Atallah as Bishop Gregorious and gave him responsibility for the Institute for Coptic Studies. Viewing it as a challenge to his authority, Bishop Shenouda sent the pope a fiery telegram: "The consecration of two bishops on one diocese is against church laws. God exists."

Wahib Attallah was born in 1919. Although he finished high school with exceptional grades, he shocked his family by refusing to enroll in the university and instead went to study at the theological seminary in 1936. He was part of the Sunday School Movement at St. Anthony Church in Shubra and shared its emphasis on spiritual revival. He entered the university in 1944 to study philosophy, and in the same year started teaching at the theological seminary. He received his M.A. in Egyptian antiquities and old languages in 1952, and then travelled to the United Kingdom, where he received his PhD from the University of Manchester in

1955, with a dissertation on the Coptic usage of Greek words. He was consecrated a monk in 1962 and then a bishop in 1967. He was a quiet man, a scholar by disposition, who never took part in the internal fights though they left their scars on him. He died in 2001.

But the greatest of the founding fathers was perhaps the one who never became a bishop. Youssef Iskandar was born in 1919 and graduated from Cairo University's Faculty of Pharmacy in 1944. He had been involved in the Sunday School Movement since 1939, and after his graduation, his pharmacy became the source of the movement's funding. Church servants passed by his pharmacy taking whatever was in its cash register. In March 1948, he sold his pharmacy, gave all the money to the church,[4] and chose to go into the Egyptian desert. He took the name Matta El Meskeen.[5] In 1954 he was chosen as the pope's representative in Alexandria. His piety and deep spirituality led hundreds who sought inner spiritual revival to flock to him; but his popularity made many of the members of the church's old guard suspicious and envious of him. He left El Sorian Monastery in 1956 and went to St. Samuel Monastery, taking thirteen monks with him. After a short four-month return to El Sorian in 1960, he left again for the deserts of Wadi El Rayan where he remained for nine years. In 1958, he established the House of Consecrated Laymen in Helwan which became a center of spiritual revival for the Coptic Church. In 1969, Pope Kyrillos sent him and his monk followers to the old, almost abandoned Monastery of St. Macarius. There he oversaw an enormous renovation project and made the monastery a model

---

4. The man who bought his pharmacy later testified that Youssef Iskandar did not retain a penny from the money he acquired from the sale, and that he had to lend him money to pay for his travel to the monastery.

5. Matta El Meskeen is translated as Matthew the Poor. Matthew the Poor was the name of the great saint and pope of the Coptic Church, Matthew I (r. 1378–1408).

for agricultural production. His work impressed President Sadat who ordered thousands of *feddans**given to the monastery. One of the greatest theologians the Coptic Church ever produced in its two-thousand-year history, he wrote 181 books. His first, *Orthodox Prayer Life*, became a guiding light to many theologians and Christians from all denominations around the world.

For Matta El Meskeen the sole mission of the church on earth was to bring sinners to Christ. He rejected the church's involvement in all non-spiritual matters be they social work or political advocacy. Such work diverted the church from its central mission. Love and giving was neither a moral nor social responsibility but an act of faith. Throughout his life he emphasized the need for every Christian to seek Christ and internal spirituality. The sole role of the clergy was to become spiritual models for their community. The only way to the revival of the early Christian church was through becoming witnesses for Christ. His utmost fear was the corruption of the monastic movement and he argued for its separation from the church's politics. He was antagonistic to the idea of the church undertaking social work and warned of the development of a patron/client dependency between the clergy and the community. Never attaining or desiring the high positions of the church, his life and work were the model for those seeking a return to the life of the great monks of the Egyptian deserts.

Not all members of the Sunday School Movement chose monastic life in the desert. Some, like Yassa Hanna, continued to serve the church as part of the laity. In 1978, Noshy Abdel Shahid established the Orthodox Patristic Center, which would translate and publish the works of the early church fathers, reintroducing Copts to works that had been long forgotten. Father Bishoy Kamel

---

* A feddan is a unit of area used in Egypt that is equivalent to 4,200 square meters.

became a priest in Alexandria and founded a true revival of Coptic life in the ancient city of St. Mark. His "Theology of the Cross" became a guiding light for generations to follow, and his church, St. George Sporting, became the center for Coptic books that reintroduced Copts to the lives of their forgotten saints. Father Salib Suryal became a priest in Giza in 1948. Together with his soul mate Bishop Samuel he played an instrumental role in the growth of the Coptic Church's social services and the establishment of the Coptic Church abroad. The Deacon's House that he established in 1955 in Giza became the training ground for the next generation of servants and leaders of the Coptic Church.

The founding fathers of the Coptic Church's revival differed in their approaches and often clashed personally and intellectually, but together they achieved a complete revolution in the Coptic Church. Replacing often illiterate priests, who were paid for providing religious services, was a generation of dynamic, well-educated priests and monks who found their rewards not in material blessings but in spiritual success. They had brought down the old order and built a new one. In 1971, two out of the three final candidates for the papacy after the death of Pope Kyrillos VI—Bishops Shenouda and Samuel—were members of that generation and the Sunday School Movement.

Why had these young men succeeded while the great pashas had failed earlier? The answer is complex. Unlike the Milli Council movement, these men had not abandoned the Coptic Church's heritage but instead embraced and celebrated it. Though they opposed certain superstitions and traditions, they never rejected the very spiritual foundation of the Coptic Church and its dogmas. They believed in miracles, celebrated the lives of saints, and sought guidance in the ancient writings of the desert fathers. Secondly, unlike the Milli Council movement, these young men involved the entire community in their struggle. This was not the battle of a few pashas against the old establishment, but a grassroots movement spanning several generations that each Copt had a part in. Their social origins helped them develop a bond to the Coptic people in a way the pashas never could. Thirdly, their revolution was not a top-down one. They infiltrated the church from below. Fourth, their success was a result of their perseverance. Unlike the Milli Council battle, this was not a onetime fight which they would abandon when demoralized. Kicked out of some churches, they went to others. Rejected in monasteries, they sought alternatives. They never abandoned the church and always sought to change it from within.

But ultimately their success was due to the giant who loomed large above them: Kyrillos VI. The Sunday School Movement could easily have ended as a failed reform movement that would end in a separation from the church, something akin to the Protestant Reformation had it not been for the guiding hand of Kyrillos VI. Kyrillos today is celebrated as a great saint of the Coptic Church, a deeply spiritual man who performed thousands of miracles. He was that and much more. The focus on his spirituality has come at the expense of his political genius. He succeeded in steering the church's ship through dangerous waters and managing the difficult transition from the old guard to the young monks. He nurtured the young monks, protecting them from the attacks of the old guard, until he handed them the leadership of the church. If Youssef Iskandar, Saad Aziz, Nazir Gayed, and Wahib Attallah were the founding fathers of the church's revival, above them all stood a great pope: Kyrillos VI.

THE PRESIDENT AND THE POPE, OR THE CLASH OF THE TITANS

Anwar El Sadat was certainly an unlikely successor to Gamal Abdel Nasser. Although Sadat had a long history of political activism and was involved in various plots before the 1952 coup, he had never distinguished himself under Nasser. Viewed as a mediocre man, his rise to the presidency was regarded as temporary by those who held the keys to power. Sadat's true qualities were not realized by Nasser's old guard until it was too late. Having crushed his internal opponents in May 1971, Sadat faced the overwhelming challenge of trying to find a way out of the predicament Egypt was in after its humiliating defeat by Israel in 1967. After some hesitation, he finally moved forward by launching an attack on Israel on October 6, 1973. The initial success of the Egyptian war effort gave the country a new sense of pride and its leader a much needed legitimacy.

As president of Egypt, Sadat initiated a break with Nasser's policies. Lacking any commitment to a long-term struggle against Israel and realizing the futility of such animosity and the price Egypt paid for such foreign adventures, he sought to put an end to Egypt's involvement in the Arab/Israeli conflict. His policy took him to unexpected places: from the Knesset in Jerusalem and eventually to Camp David. His alliance with the United States and peace with Israel meant an end to Egypt's alliance with the Soviet Union and a boycott by Arab states.

In internal affairs, Sadat had little passion for Nasser's socialist policies and began opening the country's economy to the world. The Egyptian state's ability to provide its part of the Nasserite bargain with the population had already shown signs of strain, and this trend continued under Sadat. While the Egyptian regime maintained its verbal commitment to socialist policies, the reality was a state bureaucracy and services network that had lost all ability to deliver due to population growth. The state's withdrawal from its active duty meant the rise of alternative networks to provide for the needy in the fields of education, health, and financial assistance. Inevitably what filled the gap left by the state were religious institutions. Both the church and the rising Islamists witnessed a wide expansion of their activities, ultimately replacing the state in providing for the people.

Sadat was no friend of democracy, but nonetheless he undertook opening up the political sphere as well. The one-party system was abolished and political parties were allowed. Sadat's notion of political pluralism was limited however. Intolerant of criticism, he envisioned a loyal opposition that would be allowed some participation but not a genuine democracy. Sadat did not dismantle the totalitarian aspects of Nasser's regime. The totalitarian foundation of the Egyptian state continued, with other entities beside the state filling that vacuum as well.

But ultimately his most important domestic decision, a decision that would eventually cost him his life, was the freedom he gave to the formation of Islamist groups. In order to counter the prevailing Nasserist and leftist domination of university campuses, Sadat allowed, and in some cases encouraged, the growth of Islamist currents on campuses and eventually beyond. More religious and conservative than his predecessor, Sadat did not realize until it was too late that he had unleashed a storm that would destroy him.

The Islamization of Egypt was now in full force. Under Nasser, the Islamization of education had begun, but it soon spread to the media. Islamic subjects began to dominate the official TV channels, radio, and government newspapers. Sadat was fond of using Islamic references in his speeches. Religion was increasingly replacing nationalism as the foundation of the country; Christianity was ridiculed daily in the press. It was only inevitable that this would alienate Copts, who were increasingly fearful for their future. On university campuses, Islamist groups began targeting Christian students. Clashes soon took place. More violence became only a matter of time.

The focal point of some attacks was buildings that Christians used for prayer and that had not obtained the necessary government

approval. On November 6, 1972, an attack took place in El Khanka
on such a building. Angered, Pope Shenouda ordered some bishops and priests to march to the place and hold Mass. Such a march
was viewed as a provocation by Muslims, and the building was
attacked again. The parliamentary committee tasked with investi-
gating the attack noted that out of 1,442 church buildings in Egypt
only 500 had the necessary governmental approval. It also noted
that in the ten-year period from 1962 to 1972, 127 permits were
given to church buildings and that only sixty-eight of these were
for the Coptic Church. These sixty-eight included only twenty-
two new and forty-six renovation permits. The committee recommended a government solution to the problem, but none was
undertaken.

The number of attacks increased. A church in Cairo was burned
in 1979 and on August 4, 1981, another was bombed, leaving three
dead. Attacks on priests were on the rise and a number of churches
in Alexandria were bombed in January 1980. Islamist groups had
obtained a fatwa from one of their religious leaders that any Copt
who donated money to churches was a legitimate target for rob-
bery. The sectarian clashes reached an epic high point in June 1981
in El Zawya El Hamra district in Cairo where for three days the
killing went on with little police efforts to stop the violence that
left eighty-one Copts dead.

The state and the Islamists competed on suggesting more laws
that would guarantee the Islamization of the country. Al Azhar
proposed a law in 1977 for the implementation of shari'a in the
country. The law included the implementation of the Islamic penal
code and the death penalty for apostates. On March 21, a court
ruled that shari'a was to be applied to Copts in their personal
status cases, allowing men to marry four women and obtain
divorce. The personal status law governing Copts was already a
problem since Nasser's abolishment of the religious courts in 1955.

Under law 462 of 1955, the application of non-Muslim personal status laws was limited only to those cases where the two parties belonged to the same sect. Furthermore this involved only marriages and divorce. In all other issues, such as guardianship, inheritance, adoption, and legal capacity, Islamic shari'a was applied to all Egyptians.

The Muslim Brotherhood's magazine *El Daawa* published endless articles against Copts. The anti-Coptic themes introduced by Ahmed Lutfi El Sayed in the Egyptian Conference in 1911 had never completely disappeared but they reappeared more forcefully in the Brotherhood's mouthpiece. Copts were the happiest minority in the world, it argued, and had no reason to complain. Copts should be content with their privileged position as *dhimmis* until, of course, they ultimately saw the light and converted to Islam. In fact, Copts were not being discriminated against in Egypt but were favored by the state. Copts were attempting to change the face of Egypt by building more churches than they actually needed. Copts were a fifth column that aimed to subvert the country. Rumors of Copts stockpiling weapons were widespread. A forged report of a secret meeting between Pope Shenouda and priests in Alexandria in 1972 was extensively distributed. It gave birth to the Islamist myth that everything had been fine in Egypt between its Muslims and Christians until Shenouda became pope. According to the report, which ran along the lines of the Protocols of the Elders of Zion, it was claimed that the pope told his secret audience that Egypt would be re-Christianized just as Spain had been. Copts should have many children while making sure to decrease the fertility rate of Muslim women. The conspiracy theories resulted in Copts being discriminated against in the field of gynecology. Other departments in universities were not spared. It was becoming impossible for any Christian to obtain the necessary grades to be appointed lecturer in the university. Discrimination against Copts in government cooperatives and the bureaucracy became wide-spread. Hardly any Copts were elected to the Egyptian parliament and Copts were scarce in the top positions in government.

No church leadership could stand by and watch idly as such an assault took place, and certainly not one led by Pope Shenouda. Some of the other bishops, most importantly among them Bishop Samuel, were afraid that undertaking a forceful response would result in a backlash against Copts, and instead argued for using intermediaries from the old Coptic elite and petitioning the president for protection. For its part, the Coptic elite had accepted dhimmitude and feared any reaction from the church. Pope Shenouda would have none of that. In the face of Copts flocking to the church for protection, he opened its gates to them. The church had to assert itself and defend the collective rights of Copts. True, Christ had taught forgiveness of transgressions, but that was only in personal cases. No one had the right to forgive collective transgressions, Shenouda reasoned. It is left to history to judge which approach was wiser, but it was only natural for Copts to side with their pope and his stand. The Coptic elite had become completely separated from the plight of their brethren and grew delusional as to the dimension of the challenge they faced. At their moment of crisis, Copts chose Shenouda as their hero.

Alexandria had been an early focal point in the clash with Islamists. Its priests naturally took the lead in defending Copts against the Islamist onslaught. In July 1972 the priests of Alexandria gathered at a conference and declared that Copts preferred martyrdom to giving up their faith. They begged the state to protect their rights and their religion from the Islamist attacks. Their pleas went unanswered. On December 16, 1976, as a result of the push for the implementation of shari'a and especially the apostasy laws, the second Coptic Conference in Egyptian history gathered.

Exemplifying the change the Coptic community had undergone, this time around it was the church and not members of the laity that was at the forefront in organizing and leading the conference. The conference issued eight demands. It demanded the protection of religious freedom and rejected attempt of forced conversion to Islam and the implementation of the apostasy law. It rejected the imposition of shari'a on Copts in their personal status cases, viewing it as a threat to the foundation of the Christian family. It demanded an end to discrimination and equality in employment and parliamentary representation. It also asked the state to take appropriate measures to deal with extremists and put an end to their attacks on Copts. Concluding its deliberations, it urged that all Copts fast for three days and pray for God's intervention to save them from their plight. The Coptic Conference was followed by an Islamic one in July 1977. Unlike its predecessor in 1911, this conference did not aim to hide its agenda in name or substance under the guise of nationalism. It bluntly demanded the complete implementation of shari'a.

The pope wrote a memorandum to the presidency on August 30, 1977, objecting to the proposed implementation of the apostasy law. In September 1977 the Holy Synod announced another three-day fasting for God to intervene. Twice delegations from the Holy Synod met with high-ranking Egyptian officials to plead for an end to the discrimination Copts faced. In face of the complete silence of the state to their pleas and an increase in the number and potency of the attacks they were subjected to, Pope Shenouda announced on March 26, 1981, that he would not receive any state representative sent bearing congratulations for the Easter celebration. Instead, he was travelling to the monastery to pray for God's salvation of his people. The man who sat in the seat of St. Mark had played his hand. The response from the man who sat at the head of the Egyptian state was not late in coming.

On May 14, 1980, Sadat had delivered a fiery speech to the Egyptian Parliament. He accused the pope of seeking to establish a Christian state in the south of Egypt in Asyut. He decried what he called the church's attempt to be a state within a state, and accused Copts of aiming to provoke foreign powers against Egypt and of receiving weapons and training from the Phalangists in Lebanon. He concluded his speech with the ominous words: "I am a Muslim president of an Islamic country." Demonstrations by Copts in the United States during his visit there did not cool his temper. Irritated by the opposition in general and finally realizing the threat Islamists posed to his regime, he ordered most of Egypt's opposition leaders and members of Islamist groups arrested on September 5, 1981. Father Matta El Meskeen pleaded with him to protect the church as an institution. Sadat announced the cancellation of the presidential decree appointing Pope Shenouda. While unable to touch his religious authority, Sadat had removed him as the official representative of the church in the eyes of the state. Furthermore, he ordered the pope's confinement in the St. Bishoy Monastery. He had tens of bishops and priests arrested. He ordered the formation of a committee composed of five bishops[6] to replace the pope in managing the affairs of the church. His decisions were put to a vote in a popular referendum five days later, and the results were declared to be overwhelmingly in favor. A propaganda campaign against the pope was unleashed in the state media. While accepting Sadat's decisions, the Holy Synod and the

---

6. The committee was composed of Bishop Samuel, Bishop Gregorious, Bishop Youannes, Bishop Athanasius, and Bishop Maximous. The committee's composition was suggested by Father Matta El Meskeen.

Milli Council both declared that the pope was the spiritual head of the church and could not be replaced while he lived. One month later, on the eighth anniversary of the October war of 1973, and celebrating his greatest accomplishment among his army, Sadat was struck down by Khaled El Islamboli and his colleagues. The bullets did not take the life of Sadat alone. Bishop Samuel, who was seated among the audience, was also killed.

The church and state had collided in a way never before seen in Egyptian history. While under Muslim rule popes had largely accepted dhimmitude and fallen silent, only raising their hands in prayer as their people were persecuted, a modern pope could not ignore the screams of his people. Faced with the rise of Islamism and watching the state fail to protect its Coptic citizens, the church raised its voice. The caution and warnings of Bishop Samuel were ultimately not suitable for the times. But the clash was not only that of two institutions, but perhaps more importantly of two men. The two personalities were set on a collision course from the very start. In a sense, Egypt was too small to hold both of them. One of them had to go.

THE REVOLUTION INSTITUTIONALIZED

Pope Shenouda III (r. 1971–2012) had survived the rule of President Sadat. During his forty-year reign he managed to not only transform the church along the lines of his revivalist vision, but more importantly to institutionalize those changes making them impossible to reverse. Today's Coptic Church as an institution is built solely on his vision.

Pope Shenouda had inherited a Holy Synod composed of twenty-six bishops. Some of them belonged to the old guard and he had to move cautiously with them. Others like Bishops Samuel, Gregorious, Andrawous, and Athanasius had competing visions of how the church should be governed and where it should go. Given the Coptic understanding of the pope as merely first among equals, Shenouda had to move cautiously. The powers he had at his disposal however were not small; chief among them was the fact that he alone could consecrate new bishops. He used that weapon extensively in three ways. First, he dramatically increased the number of general bishops. He had inherited two general bishops from Pope Kyrillos and during his reign he consecrated forty-five more. Eight of these he later placed in dioceses after their previous bishops had died, thirteen he sent to serve newly established dioceses and churches abroad, and three he consecrated as heads of monasteries. Secondly, the enormous expansion of the Coptic Church abroad allowed him to create new dioceses. The Coptic Church today has seventeen official dioceses plus nine general bishops overseeing churches abroad. Thirdly and most importantly upon the death of a bishop the pope divided his diocese into smaller ones. The diocese of Sharkia was thus divided into seven smaller ones, Qena into four, and Beni Suef into five. The result was to increase the number of bishops of dioceses inside Egypt from twenty-one to forty-eight. Throughout his reign he consecrated a total of 117 bishops. Outliving all of his competitors, Pope Shenouda had time on his side. The Holy Synod of the Coptic Church is today composed of ninety-six bishops only one of whom, Metropolitan Mikhail of Asyut, was consecrated by a previous pope.

This move was not purely a political one, though without a doubt it allowed the pope absolute control of the church. The old bishops had ruled over large dioceses and some of them had had hardly any effective contact with their congregations. The expansion of the church's role in the lives of Copts and their population increase meant that smaller dioceses were required to effectively serve a growing population. Smaller dioceses allowed bishops to know all Copts they served, and to cater to their spiritual and material needs.[7] Nonetheless by virtue of his long reign and the number of bishops he consecrated, Shenouda had made the position of bishop much less powerful than it had been in the past with no individual bishop able to mount a challenge to his authority. Many of the new bishops had been the pope's disciples before entering the monastery and most shared his vision for the church. The huge expansion in the number of bishops was not however without its negative aspects as new bishops were often chosen after spending only a very short period in the monasteries.

Himself consecrated as a bishop for the theological seminary and Coptic upbringing, Pope Shenouda devoted countless hours to teaching. His weekly sermons continued to be a popular attraction for the Coptic public. He personally taught theological subjects in the theological seminaries in Cairo and Alexandria as well as abroad. He continued until his death as editor in chief of *Al Keraza* magazine and personally oversaw and edited all of its articles. He contributed endless articles to newspapers and magazines in Egypt and abroad. Through his sermons, lectures,

---

7. As an example, the church in the delta town from which my father hailed was originally part of the Giza and Qalioubia Diocese. The bishop at the time visited the area only once a year, spending a day in each of its churches. The diocese was divided into two by Pope Kyrillos and then the part to which we belong was further divided into three by Pope Shenouda. Our current bishop, Maximous, inherited fourteen churches in his diocese which have increased in number to twenty-five today. His smaller diocese and his dynamic personality have allowed him to visit our church at least once a week and visit the homes of every Copt living in the diocese at least once a year.

and articles he was able to define what Coptic Orthodoxy meant
and succeeded in sidelining all those, such as Father Matta
El Meskeen and Bishop Gregorious, who held different views on
theological matters. His detractors pointed out that, by populariz-
ing theological issues he had trivialized them and weakened the
foundations of Coptic theology.

Monasticism received the pope's utmost attention. During his
reign the number of Coptic male monasteries grew from nine to
twenty-eight, and the number of nunneries from five to seven.
Some were completely new, built in the deserts of Egypt and
abroad; others were once-abandoned monasteries which were
revived under the leadership of monks sent from active ones. The
restoration of monastic life to these monasteries allowed them to
accept new recruits and grow to a level to be officially recognized
by the Holy Synod. Monks were also sent to historic monasteries
that had been completely abandoned in order to protect them and
preserve them for the church. Growth in numbers paralleled
growth in size. Hundreds of Copts, almost all of them university
graduates with some holding master's degrees and PhDs flocked
to monasteries, choosing the life of the desert over the material
world. Today Coptic monasteries hold more than fifteen hundred
monks and six hundred nuns within their walls. Today's modern
Coptic monastery is a flourishing small city in the desert and no
longer just a place for prayers and seclusion. Each monastery
works on reclaiming desert land, growing all kinds of crops, and
raising cattle. Carpentry workshops produce wooden objects used
in churches and other workshops produce all sorts of church merchandise. Many monks are active in writing books dealing with
church history, theological issues, and the lives of saints. Other
monks serve as priests in Coptic churches abroad. The modern
Coptic monastery today is a hub of Coptic life, but the flourishing has not come without its negative aspects. Critics point to the

destruction of the life of seclusion that was once the hallmark of Coptic monasticism.[8]

Institutionalizing Pope Shenouda's vision for the Coptic Church has necessitated codifying the changes to make them permanent. In 1985, for the first time in its history, the Holy Synod organized its internal laws, created a permanent secretariat, and divided its members into permanent committees dealing with various church matters. Yearly meetings of the Holy Synod have produced a large volume of laws and decisions organizing every aspect of the church's activities. Bishops can no longer consecrate monks at their whim, consecrate those priests, or use them in their dioceses without the agreement of the monastery's bishops or the pope. Monks cannot just wander and serve outside their monasteries without the pope's prior approval. Lists of monks and applicants are kept and circulated between the monasteries, and monks are forbidden to take confessions of women. Monks serving outside their monasteries have to return after six years and spend one year in their monastery unless exempted by the pope. The monasteries were put under effective administrative control.

Services and rituals were no longer haphazard but institutionalized and systemized throughout the Coptic Church. Each church received a board of directors to manage its affairs. Hundreds of priests were consecrated by the pope for churches in Cairo, Alexandria, and abroad in order to expand services to the growing community. Priests received trainings before and after being consecrated and so did their wives. The church laws governing deacons were modernized and, for the first time in the modern history of the Coptic Church, women were consecrated as deacons. The

---

8. Monasticism, according to Coptic theology, is not merely a renunciation of earthly pleasures, but complete death from the world. Upon being consecrated a monk, the young candidate lies on the ground while the Prayers of the Dead are read over him.

newly established Bishopric of Youth was responsible for the
training of church servants. Christian groups were established in
every university department under the leadership of the Bishop of
Youth, Bishop Moses. A dynamic man, he modernized the church's
communications and outreach to youth. Summer camps were organized for church servants, youth magazines produced, sports activities and competitions created and training for church servants
systemized. An administrative apparatus was created throughout the
church and thousands of ordinary Copts were brought into church
activities and services not just as recipients but as active participants.
Everyone had a role to play and could contribute not just money but
more importantly his or her time for helping out in the expanding
social and spiritual services. The Milli Council was reestablished in
1973 though with virtually no authority and little role to play besides
approving the pope's plans. New laws concerning the sacrament of
marriage were issued with regulations requiring a minimum age for
the newlyweds and a maximum fifteen-year difference in age
between them, as well as ordering medical checkups before marriage. Books sold in Coptic Church bookstores had to be reviewed
in order to make sure they did not divert from Orthodox theology.
Special attention was given to combating the infiltration of Protestant preachers and ideas inside the Coptic Church. The Holy Synod
issued statements warning Copts not to associate with Protestant
preachers and not to attend Protestant meetings. Excommunications were issued against those Coptic priests and monks who
showed signs of endorsing Protestant theological positions.

The scope of the services provided was enormous. Though
detested by the pope, Bishop Samuel's lifelong work and passion
had finally been endorsed. By the time of his death, his vision of a
church that provided for both the spiritual and material needs of
its members had become the de facto policy of the church. Through
his enormous ecumenical network and contacts, Bishop Samuel
had managed to acquire enormous Western funding for his projects

as well as scholarships for church servants. Hospitals for the sick, literacy classes for those who could not read, libraries, small cinemas, sports clubs in every church, Sunday schools for every youngster, and vocational training for workers—the dreams of Bishop Samuel had come true as the church adopted an all-encompassing model for community development. Most of the new young bishops shared his passion and services were no longer centralized in Cairo but took a local shape in each diocese, although there were some new bishops, such as Bishop Amonious of Luxor, who had little interest in such work and remained committed to a view of the bishop's role as solely a man of prayer. Most of the others expanded in areas that went beyond Bishop Samuel's dreams such as cattle breeding and a leather factory in the diocese of Minya. Bishops who did not have Bishop Samuel's foreign contacts depended on donations from local rich families, Cairo industrialists, and finally on the growing flow of donations from Copts abroad.

The lives of Copts had become centered around their church. Copts flocked to their church seeking a life within its walls in face of a growing discrimination against them in the public sphere. Faced with the rise of Islamists in Egypt, and Copts' growing exclusion, they ran to their church seeking solace. It was a two-way street, the church expanded its services to provide for the community and the community demanded that the church provide for its growing needs. Copts went to their priests and bishops to ask for advice and guidance on everything in their lives and the church became the sole representative of the community. The doors that were opened to them inside the Cchurch in its expanding services gave them opportunities for personal and professional growth. Copts who were denied leadership positions in their country found an opportunity to occupy those leadership positions inside their churches. In face of a public sphere that suppressed and humiliated them expecting them to act as happy *dhimmis*, the church gave them self-esteem and helped them regain their lost confidence. The story was however not only that of a church growth and a community running to it out of fears of the outside world. The revival and growth of the Coptic Church was an internal story that had its roots in the Sunday School Movement and had more to do with an inner spiritual and religious revival than with an outside threat. If there was an outside instigator of that revival, the Sunday School Movement was born in response to the Protestant challenge and not the Islamic one.

Bishop Samuel's pioneering work on ecumenical relations and opening up the Coptic Church to the rest of Christianity, though ridiculed during his life and viewed with suspicion by those fearing Protestant infiltration of the church or a grand Western Zionist conspiracy to control it, was endorsed and continued by the pope after Samuel's death. The Coptic Church cemented its relationship and communion with its fellow Oriental Orthodox Churches in Antioch and Armenia with the three churches cooperating extensively and benefiting from each other's experiences. The patriarchs of the Oriental Orthodox Churches meet regularly and cooperate in dialogues with other churches. In May 1973 Pope Shenouda and Pope Paul VI issued a joint Christological declaration that solved the main point of contention between the two churches that had led to their break.[9] While a dialogue between the two sees has continued, it has stalled over various

---

9. The declaration read: "We confess that our Lord and God and Savior and King of us all, Jesus Christ, is perfect God with respect to His divinity, perfect man with respect to His humanity. In Him His divinity is united with His humanity in a real, perfect union without mingling, without commixtion, without confusion, without alteration, without division, without separation. His divinity did not separate from His humanity for an instant, not for the twinkling of an eye. He who is God eternal and invisible became visible in the flesh, and took upon Himself the form of a servant. In Him are preserved all the properties of the divinity and all the properties of the humanity, together in a real, perfect, indivisible and inseparable union."

disagreements that emerged after the separation, concerning Purgatory, Immaculate Conception, and the Proceeding of the Holy Spirit from the Son. The dialogue with the Eastern Orthodox Churches was more successful with the issuance of the joint statement between the Eastern and Oriental Orthodox Churches in their meeting in Egypt in 1989 and in Switzerland in 1990. Obstacles remain, however, regarding the acceptance of the councils held after Chalcedon and the lifting of anathemas of fourth- and fifth-century fathers by both sides and thus prevent their full communion. In 2001 the Coptic pope and the Eastern Orthodox patriarch of Alexandria agreed to accept the sacrament of marriage conducted by the other side. The ecumenical outreach started by Bishop Samuel continued with the Coptic Church actively participating in the World Council of Churches as well as the Middle East Council of Churches and the All-African Council of Churches.

However, the most important development in the history of the Coptic Church and one that would have profound implications for its future took place outside the borders of Egypt. In the second half of the '50s the first substantial wave of emigration by Copts to the West took place. The first wave was composed of highly qualified professionals who were seeking a better future. Following Nasser's socialist policies in 1961, a second wave of Copts, composed of members of the upper middle class and upper class, left and joined the first immigrants in the West. The rise of Islamists in the '70s led to a third wave emigrating to escape an Egypt that was becoming alien to them. Emigrants of the third wave were more diverse in background and economic and social standing and included many poverty-stricken Copts. The continuous drain of Copts from Egypt only intensified in the following years. Another wave of emigration was not permanent in nature and involved Copts emigrating to the Gulf States and Libya to take part in the building of the booming economies in those countries after the oil shocks in 1973 and 1979.

The Coptic Church was facing a serious crisis. It was suddenly tasked with caring for the spiritual needs of those Coptic emigrants and it had no means at its disposal to deal with such a challenge. The burden fell on the shoulders of Bishop Samuel and he proved up to the challenge. Bishop Samuel travelled across the globe visiting Coptic emigrants, providing them with sacraments and most importantly organizing their communities in order to build churches. He used his extensive contacts with Western churches to acquire funds to help those communities build their first churches. He arranged for priests from Egypt to travel abroad to provide for those Copts' spiritual needs and kept sending them pastoral letters and following their work and lives. In 1964, the first priest specially consecrated for serving Copts abroad, Father Morcos Morcos, was sent to Toronto and another priest was sent to live in Germany for a year to serve Copts there. In 1961 the first Coptic Church was established in the Gulf in Kuwait. In 1969, a priest was sent to Australia and, in 1973, Father Antonious Henin was sent to Los Angeles. The first churches were rented from Protestant and Catholic churches until Copts could collect enough money to build their own. Priests started building churches, and when Pope Shenouda ascended to the papacy in 1971 there were seven established Coptic churches abroad in Jersey City, Los Angeles, Sidney, Melbourne, Toronto, Montreal, and London. Those first churches were carved in the rock with few resources and enormous obstacles.

Under Pope Shenouda the increase in the number of emigrants meant a dramatic increase in the number of churches. Father Salib Suryal travelled to Germany in 1975 and within two years had established seven Coptic churches and, two years later, a Coptic monastery there. By 1976 there were seventeen churches in the United States alone, and by 1995 that number had grown to fifty-seven. By 1995, Australia had twenty-three Coptic churches, Canada thirteen, and forty-five were spread across Europe. Today the Coptic Church has a whopping 202 churches in the United States, fifty-one in Canada, forty-seven in Australia, and twenty-nine in the United Kingdom. More than a hundred churches are spread across Europe in Germany, the Netherlands, France, Austria, Italy, Sweden, Denmark, Switzerland, Ireland, and Hungary. In Asia and Oceania, there are churches in Japan, New Zealand, Fiji, Thailand, Singapore, Hong Kong, China, Malaysia, South Korea, Taiwan, and Pakistan. Today there are also Coptic churches in Brazil and Bolivia, each with its own bishop. The Coptic Church is no longer just the Church of Egypt, but is now a worldwide church that serves its adherents across the globe.

The building of churches was the least of the challenges the Coptic Church faced in serving Copts abroad. The entire liturgy and history of the Coptic Church had to be translated into the languages of the countries where Copts now lived so that a second generation, who were not well versed in Arabic, could understand the church's rituals. Many of the Copts emigrating to the West had married Western women, and priests were forced to deal with thorny issues related to recognizing marriages performed in non-Coptic churches, civil marriages, divorce cases, and the baptism of children. For the first time, the church was faced with the challenge of atheism, one it had never faced before and didn't know how to tackle. Finding appropriate priests to serve was another challenge. These priests were not only required to be familiar with the languages of the countries they were sent to, but also equipped to deal with congregations that had been influenced by the freedoms of the West and its habits. The church was suddenly faced with challenges such as how to deal with widespread drug and alcohol use. Pope Shenouda was fond of repeating that a church without youth was a church without a future. Keeping the second generation Copts and tying them to their mother church was the greatest test. New methods had to be invented to address Westernized Copts. The challenge was not only in keeping them Christian in face of an atheist challenge, but also to keep them Egyptian and Coptic with all the things that entailed. New immigrants proved to be a further burden on the already stretched to-the-limit capacity of the Coptic churches abroad. New immigrants, especially ones with fewer skills and financial capabilities were completely dependent on the church not just for spiritual needs but also for all kinds of social needs. The churches abroad became hubs providing all kinds of services from Arabic language classes to selling Egyptian food in their supermarkets. Eventually Coptic schools as well as six theological seminaries were built in the West to keep the Coptic faith alive. Monasteries were established to open the door for monastic life to Copts abroad. Today the Coptic Church has twelve Coptic bishops with dioceses in the West as well as four Coptic general bishops with many of the churches abroad still under the direct control and supervision of the pope himself. Pope Shenouda undertook numerous trips to the West to visit Copts abroad, consecrate priests for them, bless their churches, and strengthen their bond with the motherland. By 2003 he had visited the United States twenty-eight times, the United Kingdom twenty-six, Canada eleven, and Australia six times.

The expansion of the Coptic Church outside the boundaries of Egypt was not only the result of Copts emigrating. In 1974, a group of French who adhered to Orthodoxy was seeking to join one of the established Orthodox churches. After examining their faith and its compatibility with Coptic theology, they joined the Coptic Church, with their leader being consecrated bishop. In 1994, a group of British Orthodox, who had lost their relation with Orthodox churches, similarly sought to join the Coptic Church. The British Orthodox Church, which is governed by a metropolitan separately from the Coptic community in Britain, today is compromised of eleven churches and a few thousand members. Similarly, the political separation between Ethiopia and Eritrea has resulted in the establishment of a separate Eritrean Orthodox Church which has sought to operate as a separate body under the Coptic Church. Pope Shenouda consecrated the first five Eritrean bishops in 1993 and its first patriarch in 1998. The Coptic Holy Synod has within its ranks two Eritrean bishops who serve Eritrean immigrants in the United States and the United Kingdom.

But the most startling story of the growth of the Coptic Church was in its missionary work in Africa. Since Mohamed Ali's invasion of Sudan, the Coptic Church had maintained a presence there with bishops in Khartoum and Atbara. In 1949, a message was received from a group in South Africa who sought to join the Coptic Church. A bishop was consecrated for them, but due to political problems between Egypt and the apartheid regime there, the South African government refused to renew his residence in the country. The Coptic missionary work in the African continent would have to wait for another quarter-century. In 1976, Pope Shenouda consecrated Bishop Antonious Morcos as a general bishop for Africa. Through enormous dedication and hard work, Antonious Morcos was able to start Coptic churches in numerous African countries starting with Kenya. In 1995, Bishop Boulos was consecrated as bishop for evangelism and missionary work in Africa. Today the Coptic Church has more than sixty-five churches across Africa in Botswana, the Democratic Republic of Congo, Ghana, the Ivory Coast, Kenya, Lesotho, Namibia, Nigeria, South Africa, Swaziland, Tanzania, Togo, Zambia, and Zimbabwe. With its history free of the colonialism that many of the Catholic and Protestant churches were tainted with in the eyes of Africans, the Coptic Church proved to have strong appeal. The fact that it was an African church itself which had been established by one of Christ's disciples worked in its favor. Today more than half a million Africans in sub-Saharan Africa belong to the Coptic Church.

Pope Shenouda was larger than life, both in his virtues and vices. His personality impacted every corner of the Coptic Church and the church today is the product of his vision and work. His reign witnessed the ultimate clash between the state and the church and the evolution of a working formula between them under President Hosni Mubarak. At the moment of crisis facing the Coptic community with the rise of the Islamist threat, Pope Shenouda emerged as their undisputed leader. Nasser's policies had managed to destroy the secular leadership of the community and only the church remained as the true representative of its adherents. For millions of Copts, the pope was the only father and leader they had ever known. While at the end of the day solving the Copt's predicament was beyond his means, he was able to give them a new sense of pride and purpose in serving their ancient faith. His absolute success was inside the church where he succeeded in sidelining his competitors and removing his opponents. A strong-headed man who never accepted criticisms to his approach, he shaped the church to his vision and will.

A New President and a New Challenge

Hosni Mubarak replaced Sadat at the helm of the Egyptian state in 1981. Fouad Ajami brilliantly described him in a 1995 *Foreign Affairs* article as "a civil servant with the rank of president." In the tumultuous 1940s, when every young man joined a secret organization, Mubarak had stuck to the barracks as a non-politicized officer not taking sides in the internal army battles of the '50s and '60s, and rose in military rank as any competent officer would. A man who lacked the grandiosity of his two predecessors, he chose to move cautiously handling the responsibility thrown upon his shoulders in a bureaucratic manner by not making any major decisions and dealing with political questions as merely technocratic decisions.

Mubarak's immediate task was to defuse the bomb Sadat had planted with his mass arrests of opposition figures across the political spectrum and deal with the Islamist insurgency that followed Sadat's assassination. In the long run, he needed to start a rapprochement with the Arab countries that had boycotted Egypt, uphold the peace treaty with Israel, and find a solution to Egypt's growing economic ills. Among his list of priorities, the Coptic problem was near the bottom, if it existed at all.

Less than two months after assuming the presidency, Mubarak started releasing members of the opposition. Unlike Sadat's confrontational approach during his last years, he allowed the opposition some room to breathe and a limited participation. Through those measures he hoped to be able to defuse the political crisis. Dealing with the Islamists proved to be tougher. Those who were immediately responsible for the assassination of Sadat were tried and killed, but others were released after short prison stints, though not before they endured the security's torture machine. His initial mistake was to haunt him later.

The one person who lingered on in confinement was Pope Shenouda. Bishops and priests were released but some of them were prevented from returning to their dioceses and parishes for some time. Shenouda remained banished until January 3, 1985, when Mubarak issued a presidential decree reinstating him as Coptic pope. The man who emerged from the walls of St. Bishoy Monastery was not the same fiery pope who had traded blows with Sadat but a broken man. While the pope never forgave his enemies inside the church and slowly took his revenge against those who still lived such as Father Matta El Meskeen and Bishops Gregorious and Athanasius as well as tarnishing the image of Bishop Samuel, his new policy of keeping good relations with the state baffled many observers. Some argued that his years of confinement had broken his will, while others stressed the expanding Islamist threat as a reason behind his new thinking. Faced with a much greater threat in the Islamist insurgency than the state's discrimination, the pope was forced to choose the lesser of two evils and put his bets on the state. The pope initiated the practice of Ramadan dinners in which he hosted government and Islamic dignitaries in celebration of the Muslim month of fasting. The practice soon spread in every diocese. During presidential referendums on Mubarak in 1993 and 1999, the Holy Synod issued statements declaring its support for his leadership. With even the "liberal" Wafd party allying itself with the Muslim Brotherhood during the 1984 parliamentary elections, who could blame him?

The Islamist insurgency in the south of Egypt during the '90s far surpassed any other threat Copts had been subjected to in modern times. As the government lost effective control of the south, Copts were left at the mercy of Islamist groups. Numerous large attacks left tens of Copts dead in Abu Qurqas (1990), Manfalout (1990), Imbaba (1991), Temma (1992), Asyut (1994), Kafr Dimiana (1996), El Badary (1996), Abu Qurqas (1997), and Ezbet Daoud (1997). In many villages in the south, Copts were required to pay the *jizya* and those who didn't met violent deaths. Coptic jewelry stores were a prime target of attacks by Islamists seeking avenues to finance their operations. Though unnoticed at the time, the severity of the attacks led to a massive Coptic emigration from the south to the suburbs and slums of Cairo. Some managed to escape further—to the West.

The government met the insurgency with massive violence. Hundreds of Islamists were killed and thousands arrested and tortured. But more important in the long run was the government's attempt to out-Islamize the Islamists. Mubarak's government aimed to take control of Islam and monopolize it for its goals. By entering a competition on who was more Islamic, the government, without realizing it, was helping the Islamists' cause and further Islamizing Egyptian society. The main tool in the hands of the government was the official religious establishment represented by Al Azhar. In order to win over the conservative institution, the power of Al Azhar was increased, giving it the right to confiscate and ban books deemed deviant from the official interpretation of Islam. While the move aimed to target Islamist writings, secular writers paid the heaviest price. Islamic messages increased in the media and in educational textbooks. While the educational policy was later reversed, the damage was already done. Textbooks could be changed, but the minds of teachers could not.

While the Islamist insurgency was eventually defeated by force, more problematic for Copts was the increase in random mob violence by non-politicized Egyptian citizens against them. The increased participation of their neighbors and coworkers in violent attacks against them alarmed Copts the most. A massacre in El Kosheh on January 2, 2000, which left twenty-one Copts dead after three days of uncontrolled mob violence, was a prime example. Mob attacks often started after a rumor of a church being built, a sexual relation between a Christian man and a Muslim woman, or a supposed insult to Islam at the hands of a Copt. The details of each attack varied but the end result did not. These attacks always resulted in homes burnt, shops looted, and the police forcing a reconciliation session that meant no perpetrator was ever put on trial and punished. The mob had good reason to believe that it could attack Copts with no reprisal.

The building of churches remained a thorny issue. To build a new church, renovate an old one, or even install a toilet in one, a presidential decree was required. Even when such approval was granted, local authorities put obstacles in the way to ensure the church was never built. If Copts in a village were lucky and all approvals were granted, the security apparatus easily stopped the building citing security concerns. During the period 1988 to 1998, 130 permits were granted for building churches and only fifty-seven of these to the Coptic Church. With the end of the Islamist insurgency, Mubarak was willing to be more accommodating to the Coptic plight. In 2000, permits for thirty-five new churches and two hundred for renovations were granted. In 2005, Mubarak delegated governors the authority to handle renovation petitions while retaining the authority over the building of new churches. While in some governates, his decision helped ease the situation for Copts, in others the fanaticism of local officials ensured that little was done to solve the problem. Copts continued to be under-represented in all elected and governmental positions. There were no Coptic university presidents, deans of departments, or heads of public companies. Coptic representation in the military and police force was capped at a bare minimum. In 2002, Mubarak made another gesture towards Copts by returning most of their confis-cated endowment land and declaring Coptic Christmas as a national holiday.

The last years of Mubarak's rule witnessed a significant opening of the political and media spheres in the country. Pressured by President George W. Bush's Freedom Agenda, the Egyptian regime was forced to allow the opposition more political space. The politi-cal and media opening helped shed some light on the Coptic prob-lem and the discrimination Copts faced though it resulted in no practical solutions. The Egyptian state insisted there was no Coptic problem and Islamists shared that sentiment and maintained that Copts were the luckiest minority in the world. Others resorted to leftist interpretations that aimed to portray the Coptic problem as one of class discrimination. Some members of the Coptic elite continued to deny the existence of the problem consoling themselves that the discrimination and persecution remained rampant in faraway villages and hoping that their denial might help them continue living peacefully. Their fantasies were of little help as the attacks kept occurring closer to their doorsteps. The Egyptian elite in general continued to live in a state of denial arguing that everyone suffered equally under Mubarak. Politicians and academics lamented a golden age under Egyptian liberalism before the arrival of money and Wahabist ideas from Saudi Arabia and the Persian Gulf states when there was no Coptic problem, an age that existed only in their imagination.

The Bitterness of Leaving, the Peril of Staying

The fall of the Mubarak regime in February 2011 unleashed a monumental and contagious wave of optimism. Images of Christians and Muslims holding hands in Tahrir Square were broadcast around the world and gave credence to the narrative that a new more liberal and democratic Egypt was being born. The truth was entirely different.

Copts were never enthusiastic about the revolution. Perhaps it was the wisdom of centuries of persecution that taught minorities the eternal lesson of survival: that the persecuting dictator was always preferable to the mob. The ruler, after all, could be bought off or persuaded to back off, or constrained by foreign powers, but with the mob, you stood no chance. Some of the Coptic youth were lured by the promise of a liberal Egypt in which their plight might finally come to an end, but the older generation knew better. The promises of January 2011 soon gave way to the reality of May, when the churches of Imbaba were attacked, and October, the time of the Maspero massacre. The complete collapse of the police and the state's repression apparatus liberated Islamists from any constraints. On the national level, Islamists soon swept elections and dominated the political sphere, and on the local level, Islamists, much more emboldened by the rise of their brethren nationally and the collapse of the police were asserting their power on Egyptian streets and villages and enforcing their views. While their leaders such as the Muslim Brotherhood's Deputy General Guide, Khairat El Shater, were proclaiming their goal of the "Islamization of life," local Islamists were making that goal a reality on the ground.

Patterns of persecution continued after the revolution and were reinforced. The number and scope of the attacks swelled dramatically and they were no longer limited to obscure villages or shantytowns but spread to the streets of Cairo and in front of the official TV headquarters. Church buildings were attacked and burned, mob violence against Copts was on the rise, and the new horror of forced evacuations from villages was becoming more common. Copts in small villages were increasingly forced to adhere to the Islamists' standards and vision enforced on the ground. Accusations of blasphemy and insulting religion rose with Copts as their primary targets. Seven Copts today linger in Egyptian prisons as a result of court verdicts due to such accusations. The most worrisome aspect for Copts remains the participation of their neighbors, coworkers, and people they had grown up with in attacking them. Even if the Egyptian state ruled by the Muslim Brotherhood miraculously decided to intervene, the local hatreds are now impossible to contain.

On the national level the picture is also gloomy. While the Muslim Brotherhood paid lip service to Western and Coptic concerns before its ascent to power promising equality and freedom for all, once it came to power, those promises were forgotten. The dynamics of Egyptian politics and the rise of the Salafis and the threat they pose to the Muslim Brotherhood ensure that the Muslim Brotherhood will not attempt to address Coptic grievances. The Muslim Brotherhood still insists on using sectarian rhetoric that inflames local angers against Copts, and its leaders use Copts as scapegoats for the problems Egypt faces from train accidents to opposition demonstrations. The new Egyptian Constitution, passed in December 2012, further enshrines both the Islamic nature of the state and second class status for Copts.

The Islamists' goal is not the annihilation of Copts. Copts are not likely to face a holocaust in the future, though local pogroms are all but guaranteed. The Islamists' goal is to subjugate Copts to their notions of their proper place as *dhimmis* under benevolent Islamic rule. It is for Copts to accept dhimmitude, live by it, and embrace it. Copts will be allowed to live in Egypt, tolerated as second-class citizens recognizing and accepting their second-class status. Any attempt by Copts to break those chains of dhimmitude and act as equals is frowned upon as an affront to the supremacy and primacy of Islam in its own land.

Indisputably, there is today a Coptic nation. It is however not a nation that seeks to achieve independence and statehood. That nation is not racial nor, after the loss of the Coptic language, is it based on a distinct language or on purely religious lines. Instead, it is a nation that is founded on the unique history of a church. It is a nation, as S.S. Hassan described it, whose topography is invisible. The nature of the dangers facing that nation have varied throughout its history from assimilation in an imagined liberal Egypt, to the erosion of Coptic uniqueness, the threat of Protestant missionaries, and of modernity and its discontents. Today, this nation faces a more serious threat. It can fight back against persecution although overwhelming odds lined up against it assure its defeat. It can accept dhimmitude and live as second-class citizens, or it can withdraw inside the walls of its ancient church finding comfort within those walls.

The prospects for Copts in Egypt are, to say the least, bleak. Their options are limited. Copts are not geographically concentrated in one area so that the potential for a safe haven may be considered, and unlike the Jewish emigrants escaping Egypt in the '40s and '50s, for Copts driven out of their ancestral homeland there is no Israel to escape to. Nor does their overall percentage in Egypt allow them to play a key role in shaping its future. The only option in front of them is to pack their bags and leave, putting an end to two thousand years of Christianity in Egypt. A new wave of Coptic emigration has already started and it is immense.[1] Most are heading to the countries their brethren settled in past decades: the United States, Canada, and Australia. Richer Copts are buying houses in Cyprus and with it receiving residence there, while Georgia is becoming a favored destination for their poorer brethren. The sad reality, however, is that not all of them will be able to flee. There is simply no place in the West for millions of Coptic immigrants. In the end, those Copts with better English and skills will be able to escape, leaving their poorer brethren behind. The community will lose its best elements, those who provide jobs for their brethren, those who donate to the church, further elevating its misery.

The feeling of sadness and distress is impossible to overcome as I watch the faces of the new immigrants in my church in Virginia. A church that has withstood diverse and tremendous challenges is now threatened in its very existence. When Copts leave Egypt, it is not only a loss to them and their church. A country and region will lose a portion of its identity and history. Devoutly religious, Copts point to the promises of the Lord in Isaiah 19:19 of the altar to the Lord in the heart of Egypt, and to the Coptic Church's history. Coptic history has been an endless story of decline and despair, but it has also been a story of survival, endurance in the face of persecution, and the courage and blood of martyrs becom-

---

1. I attend a Coptic church in Fairfax, Virginia. Before the revolution the church served a community of three thousand immigrant Copts. Since the revolution my church has welcomed fifteen to twenty new immigrant families per month. The total number of new Coptic immigrants in my church is now over one thousand.

ing the seeds of the church. Persecution has taken its toll on the church and on Copts, but Coptic history has also been a story of triumph amidst despair and of the Lord's protection of his people. Under the Coptic Cathedral in Cairo are the relics of two men: St. Mark, who brought the message of Christ to the Egyptians and ultimately shed his blood on its soil, and St. Athanasius, the defender of faith and the man who stood against the whole world and kept the Orthodox faith alive. It is as if the cathedral and the whole Coptic Church stands on those two pillars, martyrdom and faith.

Pope Tawadros II who rose to the throne of St. Mark on November 18, 2012, faces enormous challenges. He has declared his intention to focus on organizing the Coptic Church internally and has already undertaken some very positive initiatives in that regard but, no matter what his intentions are, he will inevitably find himself forced to deal with the growing plight of his people.

The Coptic exodus from Egypt will pose a colossal challenge to the Coptic Church. Today the Coptic Church has more than 550 churches outside of Egypt. At a moment in the not so distant future, the center of gravity of the Coptic Church will no longer be inside Egypt's borders. The nature of this challenge is one the church has never faced before and is currently ill-equipped to address: how to become a truly universal church and open up the Coptic Church to the rest of Christendom while maintaining its uniqueness; how to keep both the Christian faith of the new immigrants who will move to Western countries and the specific Coptic identity in face of an open market competition between Christian denominations; what does being Coptic actually mean for those living outside of Egypt's borders; how to provide for the material needs of the new immigrants who cling to the church not only seeking spiritual guidance; and how to cater to the ones who remain and whose lives will be increasingly difficult. These are all open questions that await history's judgment.

Books in Arabic:

Abdel Malek, Anwar. *Egypt's Renaissance: The Formation of Thought and Ideology in Egypt's National Renaissance.* Cairo: Dar El Kotob wa Al Wathaeik Al Qawmeya Press, 2011.

Abdel Sayed, Anthony Sorial. *The Self-Independence of the Ethiopian Church: A Study of the Negotiations that Took Place between the Coptic and Ethiopian Churches, 1941–1959.* Cairo: Dar El Geel Lel Teba'a, 1994.

Afifi, Muhammad. *Religion and Politics in Contemporary Egypt: Father Sargious.* Cairo: Dar Al Shorouk, 2001.

Al Ahram Center for Political and Strategic Studies. *The State of Religion in Egypt Report, 1995.* Cairo: Al Ahram Center for Political and Strategic Studies, 1996.

Atiya, Aziz Suryal. *A History of Eastern Christianity.* Cairo: Maktabet El Mahaba, 2005.

Atiya, Mounir. *Anba Gregorius: The Biography.* Cairo: Sons of Bishop Gregorius, 2002.

Badawy, Gamal. *The Sectarian Strife in Egypt: Its Roots and Causes.* Cairo: Al Markaz El Arabi Lel Bahth wal Nashr, 1980.

Bahr, Samira. *Copts in Egyptian Political Life.* Cairo: Maktabet El Anglo Al Masreya, 1984.

Bishay, Alice Iskandar. *Contemporary Coptic Monasticism.* Cairo: Dar Maria Lel Teba'a, 2008.

Bishop Antonious Morcos. *Come to us and Help us.*

Bishop Dioscorous. *Brief History of Christianity.* Cairo: Maktabet El Mahaba, 2003.

Bishop Youannes. *History of the Coptic Church after the Council of Chalcedon*. Cairo: Coptic Theological Seminary.

Bishop Youannes. *The History of the Coptic Church during the French Invasion on Egypt*. Cairo: Coptic Theological Seminary, 2004.

Butcher, Louisa. *The Story of the Church of Egypt*. Cairo: Maktabet El Mahaba, 2004.

Coptic Theological Seminary. *Coptic Orthodox and the Protestant Soul Salvation Organizations*. Cairo: Coptic Theological Seminary, 1962.

El Bishri, Tarek. *Muslims and Copts in the Framework of the National Group*. Cairo: Dar Al Shorouk, 2004.

El Bishri, Tarek. *The Political Movement in Egypt: 1945–1953*. Cairo: Dar Al Shorouk, 2002.

El Desouki, Assem. *The Large Landlords and Their Role in Egyptian Society 1914–1952*. Cairo: Dar Al Shorouk, 2007.

El Fiky, Moustafa. *Copts in Egyptian Politics: Makram Ebied and His Role in the National Movement*. Cairo: Dar Al Shorouk, 1988.

El Masry, Iris Habib. *The Story of the Coptic Church*. St. George Church Sporting Alexandria & Maktabet El Mahaba.

El Masry, Sanaa. *Margins of the Arab Conquest of Egypt: Tales of Entry and Journal of Fusion*. Cairo: Al Shoua'a Lel Nashr, 2004.

El Said, Refaat. *What Happened to Egypt: Muslims and Copts*. Cairo: El Amal, 1991.

Erian, Ayman. *The Man of Reform and Righteousness*. Cairo, Dar El Horreya, 2006.

Father Athanasius El Makary. *The Eastern Churches and Their Countries: The Church of Egypt*. Cairo: Dar Nubar, 2007.

Father Bigol Basily. *Did Copts Welcome the Arab Conquest of Egypt?*

Father Filothaous. *The Orthodox Argument against the Catholic Dialect.*

Father Kyrillos El Antony. *The Era of Councils*. 1991.

Father Matthew the Poor. *Articles between Politics and Religion*. Wadi El Natrun: St. Macarius Monastery Press, 1987.

Father Matthew the Poor. *The Christian in Society*. Wadi El Natrun: St. Macarius Monastery Press, 1991.

Father Matthew the Poor. *The Detailed Story*. Wadi El Natrun: St. Macarius Monastery Press, 2008.

Father Matthew the Poor. *The Eternal Church*. Wadi El Natrun: St. Macarius Monastery Press, 2002.

Father Menasa Youhana. *History of the Coptic Church*. Cairo: Maktabet El Mahaba, 1983.

Father Metias Nasr Menkarious. *"Copts: A Struggle for Survival*. Cairo: Al Katiba Al Teybia, 2007.

Father Metias Nasr Menkarious. *The Coptic National Army: 1800–1814*. Cairo: Al Katiba Al Teybia, 2007.

Father Mikhail Guirguis. *The Historical Record of Pope Shenouda III*.

Father Paula Atiya. *Ecumenism in the Coptic Orthodox Church*. Cairo: Matba'et El Karma, 2005.

Father Salib Suryal. *Autobiography*. 1994.

Father Tadros Yacoub Malaty. *St. John Chrysostom*. Alexandria: Coptic Theological Seminary, 1980.

Fouda, Farag, Younan Labib Rezk, and Khalil Abdel Karim. *Sectarianism . . . to Where?* Cairo: Dar wa Matabea Al Mustaqbal, 2005.

Ghirbal, Shafik. *General Yacoub and Chevalier Lascaris and the Project of Egyptian Independence in 1801*. Cairo: Matbaaat El Maaref, 1932.

Guirguis, Habib. *The Orthodox Rock*. Cairo: Dar Nubar Lel Teba'a, 2001.

Hamed, Raouf Abbas. *Egyptian Parties 1922–1953*. Cairo: Dar El Kotob wa Al Wathaeik Al Qawmeya Press, 2011.

Hanaa, Reda. *The Diocese of the Coptic Church and the History of Coptic Monasteries and the Lives of Bishops*.

Khedive Abbas Helmi. *My Reign: The Memoirs of Abbas Helmi II the Last Khedive of Egypt 1892–1914*. Cairo: Dar Al Shorouk, 2006.

Marmina Society. *The Memorial Book of the Father of Reform Pope Kyrillos IV*. 2011.

Marmina Society. *The Works of Patriarchs and Bishops of the Twentieth Century*. Alexandria: 2004.

Mikhail, Ramzi. *El Wafd and National Unity in the 1919 Revolution*. Cairo: Dar El Arab Lel Boustani, 1995.

Nakhla, Kamel Salah. *The History of the Patriarchs Series.* Wadi El Natrun: Deir El Sorian, 2001.

Nasr, Amir. *Pages from the History of the Church in the Modern and Contemporary Era.* 2003.

Nasr, Amir. *The Orthodox Scholar: Bishop Isidore.* Wadi El Natrun: Deir El Sayeda El Azra'a El Baramous, 2001.

Negm, Zein El Abedeen. *Egypt During the Reign of Abbas and Said.* Cairo: Dar Al Shorouk, 2009.

Nubar Pasha. *Nubar's Memoirs.* Cairo: Dar Al Shorouk, 2009.

Rofela, Yacoub Nakhla. *History of the Coptic Nation.* Cairo: St. Mark Foundation for Coptic History Studies, 2000.

Rostom, Rasmy Abdel Malek and Ishak Ibrahim Agban. *Pope Shenouda III: The Harvest of Years.* Cairo: Dar Nubar Lel Teba'a, 2003.

Sadek, Morris. *The Trial of Pope Shenouda.* Cairo: Maktab Al Nisr lel Teba'a, 1991.

Salama, Adib Naguib. *History of the Evangelical Church in Egypt: 1854–1980.* Cairo: Dar El Thakafa, 1982.

Serag El Din, Awatef. *Ahmed Lutfi El Sayed: His Political and Social Battles.* Cairo: Dar Nahdet Masr, 2011.

Tager, Jack. *Copts and Muslims: From the Arab Conquest to 1922.*

The Holy Synod. *Coptic Monastic Renaissance.* Mariut: Deir Marmina, 2004.

The Holy Synod. *The Decisions of the Holy Synod during the Reign of Pope Shenouda III.* Cairo: 2001.

Wahida, Sobhi. *On the Origins of the Egyptian Issue.* Cairo: Dar El Kotob wa Al Wathaeik Al Qawmeya Press, 2011.

BOOKS IN ENGLISH:

Atiya, Aziz S. *Copts and Christian Civilization.* Salt Lake City: University of Utah Press, 1979.

Carter, B.L. *Copts in Egyptian Politics 1918–1952.* Cairo: The American University in Cairo Press, 1988.

Davis, Stephen J. *The Early Coptic Papacy: The Egyptian Church and its Leadership in Late Antiquity.* Cairo: The American University in Cairo, 2004.

Guirguis, Magdi and Nelly van Doorn-Harder. *The Emergence of the Modern Coptic Papacy.* Cairo: The American University in Cairo, 2011.

Hassan, S.S. *Christians versus Muslims in Modern Egypt: The Century-long Struggle for Coptic Equality.* Oxford: Oxford University Press, 2003.

Hourani, Albert. *Arabic Thought in the Liberal Age: 1798–1939.* New York: Cambridge University Press, 1983.

J. Heyworth-Dunne. *An Introduction to the History of Education in Modern Egypt.* London: Frank Cass & Co., 1968.

Kedouri, Elie. *The Chatham House Version and Other Middle Eastern Studies.* Chicago: Ivan R. Dee, 2004.

Kepel, Gilles. *The Prophet and the Pharaoh: Muslim Extremism in Egypt.* Berkeley: University of California Press, 2003.

Khalil, Elhamy. *The Making of a Diocese: The Early Years of the Coptic Orthodox Diocese of Los Angeles, Southern California, and Hawaii.* The Coptic Orthodox Diocese of Los Angeles, Southern California, and Hawaii, 2008.

Lewis, Bernard. *What Went Wrong? Western Impact and Middle Eastern Response.* London: Phoenix, 2003.

Malik, Habib. *Islamism and the Future of the Christians of the Middle East.* Stanford: Hoover Institution Press, 2010.

Meinardus, Otto. *Monks and Monasteries of the Egyptian Deserts.* Cairo: The American University in Cairo Press, 1992.

Meinardus, Otto. *Two Thousand Years of Coptic Christianity.* Cairo: The American University in Cairo Press, 1999.

Mikhail, Kyriakos. *Copts and Moslems under British Control.* Forgotten Books, 2012.

P.J. Vatikiotis. *Nasser and his Generation.* New York: St. Martin's Press, 1978.

P.J. Vatikiotis. *The History of Modern Egypt: From Muhammad Ali to Mubarak.* Baltimore: Johns Hopkins University Press, 1991.

Safran, Nadav. *Egypt in Search of Political Community: An Analysis of the Intellectual and Political Evolution of Egypt, 1804–1952.* Cambridge: Harvard University Press, 1961.

Shamir, Shimon. *Egypt from Monarchy to Republic: A Reassessment of Revolution and Change.* Boulder: Westview Press, 1995.

Swanson, Mark N. *The Coptic Papacy in Islamic Egypt: 641–1517.* Cairo: The American University in Cairo, 2010.

Tignor, Robert. *Modernization and British Colonial Rule in Egypt, 1882–1914.* Princeton: Princeton University Press, 1966.

Werthmuller, Kurt. *Coptic Identity and Ayyubid Politics in Egypt, 1218–1250.* Cairo: The American University in Cairo Press, 2010.

Wiedl, Kathrin Nina. *The Role of Copts in the National Movement in Egypt until the 1919 Revolution.* Munich: Grin Verlag, 2006.

ARTICLES:

Afifi, Muhammad. "The State and the Church in Nineteenth-Century Egypt." *Die Welt des Islams,* New Series, 39, no. 3, State, Law and Society in Nineteenth Century Egypt (November 1999): 273–288.

Ansari, Hamied. "Sectarian Conflict in Egypt and the Political Expediency of Religion," *Middle East Journal* 38, no. 3 (Summer 1984): 397–418.

Berger, Maurits. "Public Policy and Islamic Law: The Modern Dhimmi in Contemporary Egyptian Family Law," *Islamic Law and Society* 8, no. 1 (2001): 88–136.

Carter, B.L. "On Spreading the Gospel to Egyptian Sitting in Darkness: The Political Problem of Missionaries in Egypt in the 1930s," *Middle Eastern Studies* 20, no. 4 (October 1984): 18–36.

Erlich, Haggai. "Identity and Church: Ethiopian-Egyptian Dialogue, 1924–59," *International Journal of Middle East Studies* 32, no. 1 (February 2000): 23–46.

Fanous, L.A. "Sir Eldon Gorst and Copts: To the Editor," *Spectator,* June 10, 1911.

Goldschmidt, Arthur Jr. "The Butrus Ghali Family," *Journal of the American Research Center in Egypt* 30 (1991): 183–188.

Haddad, George. "A Project for the Independence of Egypt," *Journal of the American Oriental Society* 90, no. 2 (April–June 1980): 169–183.

Little, Donald. "Coptic Conversion to Islam under the Bahri Mamluks, 692–755/1293–1354," *Bulletin of the School of Oriental and African Studies, University of London* 39, no. 3 (1976): 552–569.

Middleton, J. Henry. "Copts of Egypt and their Churches," *Academy,* September 30, 1882.

Nakhla, Raphael. "The British in Egypt," *An Irish Quarterly Review* 9, no. 33 (March 1920): 101–117.

Papaconstantinou, Arietta. "Historiography, Hagiography, and the Making of the Coptic Church of Martyrs in Early Islamic Egypt," *Dumbarton Oaks Papers* 60 (2000): 65–86.

Pennington, J.D. "Copts in Modern Egypt," *Middle Eastern Studies,* 18, no. 2 (April 1982): 158–179.

Perlmann, M. "Notes on Anti-Christian Propaganda in the Mamluk Empire," *Bulletin of the School of Oriental and African Studies, University of London,* 10, no. 4 (1942): 843–861.

Philipp, Thomas. "Nation State and Religious Community in Egypt: The Continuing Debate," *Die Welt des Islams,* New Series, Bd. 28, Nr. ¼ (1988): 379–391.

Reid, Donald M. "Educational and Career Choices of Egyptian Students, 1882–1922," *International Journal of Middle East Studies* 8, no. 3 (July 1977): 349–378.

Reid, Donald M. "Political Assassination in Egypt, 1910–1954," *The International Journal of African Historical Studies* 15, no. 4 (1982): 625–651.

Rowe, Paul S. "Neo-millet Systems and Transnational Religious Movements: The Humayun Decrees and Church Construction in Egypt," *Journal of Church and State* 49, no. 2 (2007): 329–350.

Seikaly, Samir. "Coptic Communal Reform: 1860–1914," *Middle Eastern Studies* 6, no. 3 (October 1970): 247–275.

Seikaly, Samir. "Prime Minister and Assassin: Butrus Ghali and Wardani," *Middle Eastern Studies* 13, no. 1 (January 1977): 112–123.

Sheldon, Amos. "Copts as a Political Factor," *Contemporary Review* 44 (July 1883): 644–659.

Tadros, Samuel. "Religious Freedom in Egypt," *The Heritage Foundation,* Backgrounder, no. 2487, November 9, 2010.

Tadros, Samuel. "The Coptic Winter," *National Review,* Volume LXIII, no. 21, November 14, 2011.

Tadros, Samuel. "The Christian Exodus from Egypt," *Wall Street Journal,* October 11, 2012.

Takawi, Mourad. "Modernizing the Coptic Community: The Laity-Clergy Struggle for Communal Representation and the Road to the 1911 Asyut Congress," unpublished M.A. thesis, The American University in Cairo, 2012.

Watson, John. "The Transfigured Cross: A Study of Father Bishoi Kamel (6 December 1931–21 March 1979)," *Coptic Church Review* 23, no. 1 & 2 (Spring/Summer 2002).

Wood, Michael. "The Use of the Pharaonic Past in Modern Egyptian Nationalism," *Journal of the American Research Center in Egypt,* 35 (1998): 179–196.

ABOUT THE AUTHOR

SAMUEL TADROS is a Research Fellow at the Hudson Institute's
Center for Religious Freedom and a Professorial Lecturer at the
Paul H. Nitze School of Advanced International Studies (SAIS)
at Johns Hopkins University. Prior to joining Hudson in 2011,
Tadros was a Senior Partner at the Egyptian Union of Liberal
Youth, an organization that aims to spread the ideas of classical
liberalism in Egypt. His current research focuses on the rise of
Islamist movements in Egypt and its implications for religious
freedom and regional politics.

Born and raised in Egypt, he received his M.A. in Democracy
and Governance from Georgetown University and his B.A. in
Political Science from the American University in Cairo. He has
studied at the Coptic Theological Seminary in Cairo.

THE HERBERT AND JANE DWIGHT WORKING GROUP ON ISLAMISM AND THE INTERNATIONAL ORDER seeks to engage in the task of reversing Islamic radicalism through reforming and strengthening the legitimate role of the state across the entire Muslim world. Efforts will draw on the intellectual resources of an array of scholars and practitioners from within the United States and abroad, to foster the pursuit of modernity, human flourishing, and the rule of law and reason in Islamic lands—developments that are critical to the very order of the international system.

The Working Group is cochaired by Hoover fellows Fouad Ajami and Charles Hill, with an active participation by Hoover Institution Director John Raisian. Current core membership includes Russell A. Berman, Abbas Milani, and Shelby Steele, with contributions from Zeyno Baran, Reuel Marc Gerecht, Ziad Haider, R. John Hughes, Nibras Kazimi, Bernard Lewis, Habib Malik, Camille Pecastaing, Lieutenant Colonel Joel Rayburn, and Joshua Teitelbaum.

INDEX